Hiram Martin Chittenden

H. M. CHITTENDEN

A Western Epic

*Being a Selection from His Unpublished
Journals, Diaries and Reports*

*Edited with Notes and Introduction
by Bruce Le Roy*

*Washington State Historical Society
Tacoma*   *1961*

Copyright 1961

Washington State Historical Society

Tacoma, Washington

Library of Congress Catalog Number 61-64226

Of this regular edition of

H. M. Chittenden: A Western Epic

one thousand copies have been printed.

Graphic design by

Walter J. Finholm and John H. Rooney

Printed in the United States of America

by Johnson-Cox Company

Tacoma, Washington

Contents

Foreword   1

I   Biographical Notes   5

II   The Yellowstone   11

III   Journals of Western Trips   29
       Journal of Trip to Pacific Coast, December 1896   31
       Journal of Trip to Wyoming and Colorado, May 1897   43
       Journal of Trip to Jackson Hole and Idaho, August 1897   51

IV   Notes on the Reservoir Service   63

V   Historical Work   77

VI   Personal Notes — An Unfinished Autobiography   85

APPENDICES
       A Chittenden Checklist   111
       Footnotes   115
       Selected References   133
       Index   135

Illustrations

Frontispiece   Hiram Martin Chittenden

Page   1   *Castor canadensis* — The Beaver

Page   5   An American Trapper

Page 11   Hot Springs, Gardiner River

Page 14   Chittenden Bridge, Yellowstone River

Page 19   General Chittenden (left foreground) supervises first
                vehicle "ascent" of Mt. Washburn

Page 23   Entrance Gate, dedicated by President Theodore Roosevelt,
                April 24, 1903

Page 27   Missouri River Steamboat

Page 35   The Golden Gate Viaduct

Page 42   Chittenden Road, Mt. Washburn

Page 77   St. Mary's Mission, Montana

Page 85   H. M. C.'s Self-caricature

Page 88   H. M. Chittenden: U. S. Military Academy, Class of 1884

Acknowledgements

The Chittenden manuscripts, together with permission to publish, were presented to the Washington State Historical Society by the daughter and sons of the General, Mrs. James B. (Eleanor Chittenden) Cress, Hiram M. Chittenden, Jr. and Theodore P. Chittenden. The family also supplied some of the illustrations used in the book, and has been extremely helpful in checking vague points related to the General's biography.

Thanks are due to the Pacific Northwest Quarterly for permission to publish in expanded form the section of the book now called *Biographical Notes*.

Duane B. Robinson, Secretary of the South Dakota Historical Society supplied information concerning Chittenden's visit to South Dakota and the Robinson family. Richard Berner, Curator of Manuscripts at the University of Washington Library, assisted in locating lost Chittenden correspondence. The United States Military Academy Library, the Corps of Engineers of the United States Army, and the Missouri Historical Society furnished additional information. Dr. Bernard Crick, of the London School of Economics assisted the Editor with access to the records of the Historical Manuscripts Commission in England, particularly valuable in reference to the history of the American fur trade.

Robert Hitchman and John M. McClelland, Jr., provided helpful suggestions in the editing of the manuscript.

Lastly, I wish to express gratitude for the assistance of Grace O. Frederick who has been typist, proof-reader and consultant, and unfailingly patient in helping in the preparation of the book.

Foreword

Foreword

As Justice Holmes said, "A great man reperesents a great ganglion in the nerves of society, or, to vary the figure, a strategic point in the campaign of history, and part of his greatness consists of his being *there*".

Chittenden *was* there, at a given moment in history, and he had the gift of knowing opportunity when he saw it. Time after time he turned the occasions of Army assignment to historical advantage. The first assignment to the Yellowstone led to the classic book on that region. A military station in St. Louis provided the six years needed to sift the records of the American Fur Company, which resulted in his great *A History of the American Fur Trade of the Far West*. Several years of service as Secretary of the Missouri River Commission terminated in the *History of Early Steamboat Navigation on the Missouri*. His western travels and researches in the history of the fur trade era made possible the definitive *Life, Letters and Travels of Father Pierre-Jean De Smet*.

Hiram Martin Chittenden's rise to greatness was firmly in the American tradition. Boyhood on the farm, education in the village schools of western New York state, and the years at West Point followed a classic pattern of development. A natural propensity toward precise thinking was sharpened by post-graduate legal training and by the subsequent career in the United States Army Corps of Engineers.

Any explanation of General Chittenden's achievements which failed to take into account the grandeur of his vision of the frontier west would be totally inadequate. The author's talent for capturing the sweep of the westward movement was personified by the mountain men and missionaries who stride through his pages.

In compiling this collection from Chittenden's unpublished notes and journals, a selection was made of those pieces which best reflected the various stages of the historian's development. We have the double fascination of encountering for the first time not only the raw sources upon which he based his books, but also of participating, as it were, in the actual evolution of a prime historian. Chittenden's literary-historical work was always

3

closely interwoven with his professional engineering activities. The brief biographical sketch which follows will show that the Army assignments always led to the publication of books and articles on the specific regions where the author served.

Because we are most concerned with Chittenden's status as a historian of the West his articles on world peace and other major questions important to his time and place are not included in this collection. The editor found it more difficult to exclude such pieces as the General's acidulous narrative of his experiences in building the Port of Seattle, or his far-seeing argument for a Cascade Tunnel.

In transcribing from the manuscripts it was found necessary to indicate by the use of brackets where illegible or missing words occur. Footnotes have been relegated to the rear of the book. Much information of value and interest, such as Chittenden's encounters with Theodore Roosevelt, had to be placed in the Appendix. A check list of Chittenden's published and unpublished writings will also be found in the Appendix. Except for books, this check list must be considered partial, restricted as it is to articles and reports pertaining only to the West. The list of published books appears in its entirety.

One liberty has been taken with the chronological arrangement of the book. Chittenden's "Personal Notes", autobiographical memoirs of his boyhood in western New York, appears last. This delightful section *may* be skipped without the reader's losing much in terms of Chittenden's western researches. But, if you read it, permit us to say that we think you are in for a wonderful bit of *lagniappe!* Surely, too, to know the mature historian and the *man*, one cannot overlook the formative years of boyhood and adolescence. These pages, dwindling off in the middle of an uncompleted sentence, were the last Chittenden ever wrote. In the quiet wisdom of the prose one finds mellow echoes from Walden Pond. And there are moments when these reminiscences find their peers in *Huckleberry Finn*.

Perhaps this collection will help to augment the already sound reputation of Hiram Martin Chittenden, historian of the West, whose work, in the round, we recognize to be a magnificent contribution to historiography.

I

Biographical Notes

Biographical Notes

WHEN JUDGE C. H. HANFORD addressed a distinguished group who were meeting at Glacier National Park in 1925 to celebrate the Upper Missouri Historical Expedition, he spoke of General H. M. Chittenden in terms normally reserved for a national movement rather than for a single individual. The General's compass, he averred, ranged "from the state of Ohio to Puget Sound — the Great Lakes, the great rivers, harbors, forests, parks, climatic conditions, enterprises of Adventurers and Pioneers, the deeds of missionaries and benevolent endeavors to christianize as well as to civilize the wilderness".[1]

The papers of Hiram Martin Chittenden were recently presented to the Washington State Historical Society by his daughter, Mrs. Eleanor Chittenden Cress, and his sons, H. M. Chittenden, Jr., and Theodore P. Chittenden. These documents go far toward confirming the jurist's appraisal of the General. Hanford's definition might even be broadened, in terms of geography as well as accomplishment. For, from the time of his youth in western New York state, where he was born about one hundred years ago, Chittenden kept a careful record for posterity. Several diaries report the intellectual struggles and gropings toward maturity, from preparatory school through the rigors of cadet life at West Point, through a successful post-graduate study of law, and then into his army career.

The unpublished papers cover the great engineering achievements — the surveys in Yellowstone National Park, the pioneering flood control in the Missouri Valley, the building of the Port of Seattle. Diaries, journals, letters, and scrapbooks attest to the Renaissance vigor of the man. Here, too, emerges an unsuspected Chittenden, a man working toward a United Nations in the years before World War I.[2]

Chittenden's fame in Western scholarship rests upon two deservedly acclaimed classics: *American Fur Trade of the Far West*[3] and the collaboration with A. T. Richardson in *Life, Letters and Travels of Father Pierre-Jean De Smet*.[4] Both were pioneering studies in their particular areas. His *History of Early Steamboat Navigation on the Missouri River*[5] and the perennial *Yellowstone National Park*[6] may not be quite so vital, but in some respects neither has been superseded. Less well-known are his book *War or Peace*[7] and the articles published in such magazines as the *Atlantic Monthly*, *Century*, and *Forum*. Articles on national questions appeared over his byline in the New York *Herald Tribune* and the *Christian Science Monitor*.[8]

Occasionally these forays into print stirred up a wasp's nest of controversy, as when he debated American intervention with Norman Angell, prior to our entry into World War I.[9] At such times he found champions in men like David Starr Jordan of Stanford, whose correspondence with Chittenden throws an interesting searchlight upon the years immediately preceding World War I.[10] Many significant names appear in the letters: Ellery Sedgwick, Samuel Seabury, Thomas Burke, Will Irwin, Senator Wesley Jones, among others.[11]

The influence of Chittenden's pioneering in the field of Western history has been enormous. He wrote well, and what he wrote was based upon original sources. But since his efforts were pioneering, his books have been to some extent outdated. What he accomplished for his time, however, has been recognized by such eminent scholars as Frederick Jackson Turner, Ray Billington, and Grace Lee Nute. Turner characterized the *American Fur Trade of the Far West* as "excellent", and he added that the map showing Western fur-trade posts "furnished the basis for the map of western posts and trails in (his own) *Rise of the New West*".[12] Billington, in *Westward Expansion*, states that "the most useful work on the fur trade is Chittenden's *American Fur Trade*".[13] Grace Lee Nute, referring to the same work, writes that, "faulty as it is in some respects, it remains the best general account available".[14]

In *Across the Wide Missouri*, Bernard DeVoto wrote ". . . General Hiram M. Chittenden published the *American Fur Trade of the Far West*, which remains the most valuable single book about the trade and the only general history of it . . ." DeVoto also suggested that it was about time for someone to synthesize all this material (the results of recent research) and to write a modern history (of the fur trade).[15] The editor of this collection concurs most fervently. It is past time.

The scrapbooks indicate that the fur-trade book received almost instant recognition. In an unpublished memoir entitled *Historical Work*[16] the General commented upon the high praise the book had received. He also noted his immense debt to Elliott Coues. Coues, while helping Chittenden with his research on the Yellowstone, became convinced of the serious purpose and painstaking thoroughness with which the military man attacked a project. He encouraged Chittenden to make a serious study of the history of the fur trade. Chittenden estimates that he went through half a carload of records of the early fur trade while he was stationed at St. Louis. His account of the research and writing of *American Fur Trade of the Far West* is a fascinating report.[17]

Few authors are capable of an accurate self-rating, and Chittenden is no exception; but he had several interesting comments to make on individual titles. He thought that the book on the Missouri was perhaps the most interestingly written, that the work on De Smet was the most laborious, but that the actual time spent in research for that book paled in comparison with the work done on the history of the fur trade. His first book, *Yellowstone National Park*, he termed "amateurish",[18] a verdict echoed by later critics; however, no one has yet produced anything better, and the book, after having gone through numerous editions, is still in print today.[19]

Hiram Martin Chittenden enacted the great drama of the westward movement in his thinking, his life, and his writing. Born in Yorkshire, New York, on October 25, 1858, the son of William and Mary Jane (Wheeler) Chittenden, he attended preparatory schools in western New York. He was graduated from the U. S. Military Academy at West Point in 1884 and was assigned to the Corps of Engineers, customary for those in the top rank of the graduating class.[20]

Dual monuments, professional and literary, mark Chittenden's twenty-year progress to the Puget Sound country. The work on flood control in the Missouri Valley is considered a great pioneering achievement. The book on the history of navigation on the Missouri grew out of his experiences in that region. The original survey of the Yellowstone and the construction of roads and bridges there are memorialized in the Chittenden Road which traverses Mount Washburn.[21] The book on the Yellowstone, someone has said, still erupts with the same fidelity as the geysers in the Park.

Public Law 779, 84th Congress, naming the Hiram M. Chittenden Locks in Seattle, states that Chittenden was the man who, "As District Engineer in Seattle was primarily responsible for the design and construction of the Locks, and whose service did so much to promote the development and progress of the Port of Seattle".[22] Recently there has been renewed interest in building a great Cascade Tunnel joining eastern and western Washington. Chittenden first proposed this project in two pamphlets as early as 1908.[23]

The papers of Hiram Martin Chittenden (that is, the major collections) are located in three places: The Washington State Historical Society, University of Washington, and Missouri Historical Society. The University of Washington received a miscellany of letters, pamphlets, and other materials in 1925 from Mrs. Chittenden.[24] The Missouri Historical Society received the records which Chittenden employed in the preparation of the history of the fur trade.[25] The collection at the Washington State Historical Society in Tacoma consists of diaries, journals, letters, scrapbooks, diplomas, and commissions.

Despite his retirement in 1910 from the Regular Army for reasons of physical disability, Chittenden continued to pour his vast intellectual energies into such projects as the development of the Port of Seattle and professional counselling on flood control in various western states. He also labored to perfect the revisions of his major historical treatises. (Eleanor Chittenden Cress said that the General revised his work on the Yellowstone in the few months just prior to his death).[26]

At the time of his retirement from active duty in 1910, Chittenden was promoted to Brigadier General, a promotion of two grades from the rank of Lt. Colonel in the U. S. Army Corps of Engineers. In an exchange of correspondence with President William Howard Taft, he expressed gratitude for his appointment. He appended a statement that he hoped he might recover his health sufficiently to return to active duty. The President replied, "I was very glad to make the appointment because I think it only a fitting reward for the services you have rendered the United States".[27]

Hiram Martin Chittenden died in 1917 at the age of fifty-nine.[28] The heroic struggles of a lifetime of service are reflected on the face of America — her forests, her national parks, her major western ports. Most important of all, perhaps, is the legacy of classic scholarship in the field of western history he bequeathed to us which must be recognized as an outstanding pioneering accomplishment. For, after Chittenden, as after Frederick Jackson Turner, a compass and a guide to the mysteries of the "Great Frontier" were available.

Bruce Le Roy

Tacoma, Washington
April 1961

II

The Yellowstone

Editor's Notes

The first important historical work produced by Chittenden was his book *The Yellowstone National Park*. His first tour of duty in the Park from 1891-1893 provided the author with ample opportunities to explore the natural phenomena and historical backgrounds of this unique region.

Chittenden had by now completed seven years of service with the Corps of Engineers, and at the time of his assignment to the Yellowstone, had just finished two years of labor on improvements of the Missouri River above Sioux City, Iowa.[1] Several permanent engineering achievements remain of Chittenden's works in the Park: the original system of tourist roads, the Entrance Arch at Gardiner, the Golden Gate viaduct, and the reinforced concrete arch bridge over the Yellowstone River just above the Upper Falls.[2] The road which traverses Mt. Washburn (see illustration on page 42) was another major accomplishment. This road was named in honor of the builder in 1913, an act that set in motion an interesting chain of circumstances.

Among the Chittenden papers is the fading telegram from Franklin Lane, Secretary of the Interior, informing him that the Mt. Washburn road had been named Chittenden Road — this in 1913.[3] In 1959, Chittenden's daughter and her husband, Major General James B. Cress, were at Yellowstone when the great earthquake occurred. Since all the tourists were isolated within the Park for several days, General and Mrs. Cress had some unexpected time to do a little exploring. In checking, they learned that the Mt. Washburn road was *still* unnamed, at least to the knowledge of Park officials. Upon returning to California, Mrs. Cress wrote to the Washington State Historical Society requesting a copy of Franklin Lane's official telegram.[4] The documentation was turned over to the National Park Service in order that "Chittenden Road" might, at long last, appear on the official map of Yellowstone National Park.

During a second tour of duty in the Park from 1899-1906, Chittenden made the acquaintance of President Theodore Roosevelt who visited Yellowstone in May 1903 to dedicate the Entrance Arch.[5] Chittenden's portrait of the impetuous T.R. does nothing to upset the traditional conception of Roosevelt as the strenuous man-of-action who reacted in a typical way in the heady freedom of a Western setting. Later, in one of the ironic twists of history, the two strong men clashed over ideas of national conservation. This story is told in the Appendix to Chapter III.[6]

Chittenden Bridge, Yellowstone River

The Yellowstone

M Y WORK in the Yellowstone Park will stand out as perhaps most important in the construction line of anything which I have accomplished, It first came to me purely as routine of the Service. On my way back from Europe, I called at the office of the Chief of Engineers in Washington and had [a] talk with Colonel Knight who was then Chief Assistant.[1] Colonel Knight told me I had been slated for the Yellowstone. I was very much pleased at this and thanked the Colonel for the assignment.[2] He said I needn't thank him as it was purely routine. There was a hole to fill and I happened to be the first to fill it. So as I say, the assignment was in the first instance purely accidental. It never was so afterwards.[3]

I made my way to St. Paul (1891) as quickly as certain matters would permit and soon after was on the train with the doughty Major Jones of the Corps of Engineers, who, in addition to his duties at St. Paul, was officially in charge of the Park work. I was to be his representative on the ground. The Major was a peculiar character, not over-scrupulous in matters of official work, and I don't think he particularly welcomed my entrance upon the scene. He took a great deal of pains to impress upon me that his civil assistant in the Park, Lamartine, by name, was absolutely indispensable to the work, and that I must rely very largely upon his judgment. He pressed the point so far that I became a little suspicious and determined to reserve my judgment.

We struck the Park in one of the very worst rainy spells that come to that region. It was cold and bleak as anything could possibly be. I was not yet fully recovered from my illness (typhoid) of the previous Fall, and some felt that I oughtn't to risk the inclemencies of that sort of weather by attempting it from the Park. Captain Anderson, the new Superintendent, whom my later work greatly surprised, told me afterward that he expected me to last just about two weeks. A grand party was being made up to go out into the Park and determine what route was to be followed from the Geyser Basins to the Lake. We made our way to the Lower Geyser Basin where we put up with such conveniences as were at hand. (I will just add here that Major Jones and Mr. Lamartine were very much concerned about me and thought I ought not to take the risk of the trip, but I didn't propose starting my tour of duty on that basis. I insisted upon going and by judicially keeping my ears open and my mouth shut I got a pretty good drift of things before we got to the Lower Basin.)

At the Lower Basin the weather was worse than ever. However, it was finally agreed that the Major and I would remain at the Hotel while Lamartine and two or three others would make a horseback reconnaissance into the mountains in the apparent direction that they wanted to go. I had been studying the map a good deal and I asked Mr. Lamartine to examine the availability of a certain route if he found it practical to do so. He received the suggestion with ill-concealed contempt and promptly dismissed it from his mind. The party came back in due time with no information worth a row of pins, but boldly asserting that the road should go so-and-so from the Upper Basin to the Lake. With this grand accomplishment the party started back in high spirits to Mammoth Hot Springs to organize the work. After a few days delay and further caution by Major Jones as to the indispensability of Mr. Lamartine, the Major left for St. Paul and I was officially, though in the Major's opinion, nominally, in charge of the work.

And now my troubles began. Here were practically $150,000 available; very important roads to build, not a sign of a survey or even reconnaissance, or even the passage of anybody over the route to afford us a guide as to where to begin or where to go. Very fortunately, there were two excellent foremen and it was decided to organize a large party under each of these and have one begin at one end of the work and the other at the other, although nobody knew where these ends were. But it would take several days to get the parties out into the field and in the meanwhile I wasn't idle in informing myself about the situation. Lamartine was very greatly surprised when he found that I was going to take active charge in the field and his displeasure was manifest enough. Nevertheless, he learned that it was useless to argue.

Gradually our relations became more and more strained as Lamartine's authority was curtailed and he was confined to the strict duties as Assistant Engineer. The business people of the Park were overjoyed at the turn of affairs and while they said nothing openly they privately assured me of their sympathy and support. I may say that the whole affair terminated by dismissing Lamartine from the service, some three months afterwards.

The new parties being organized, I decided to accompany the one going to the west end of the Lake, and the other was sent up to the Upper Basin with Mr. Lamartine to show it where to begin work. I was later very sorry that this party got into the field as soon as it did. It was a long, tedious, sombre experience getting to the shore of the Thumb, but we finally got there, in the midst of a heavy snowstorm (although it was July), just in time to make our camp before dark. Two huge bears sauntered off as we made our way onto the shore. That evening there was the loud report of a gun in camp, and as I knew that none of our party carried weapons I called for an explanation. It appeared that some men had found a worn, rusty gun from which the stock was entirely eaten away and which had lain there for no one knows how long, someone tried the trigger and sure enough, the gun was loaded and went off without bursting. I have since regretted that I didn't keep that as a relic.

Next morning our work began in earnest. It seemed plain enough to me where our starting point should be. I then, as early as possible, made a reconnaissance with Mr. Askey, a very able foreman, back for a mile or so, up the hill and after some little examination, we decided that we could proceed in safety at least thus far. So on the part that we had staked out, I took one or two good men and proceeded to extend the survey to the Continental Divide, some three or four miles distant. My only instrument was a hand level and a strong stick, five feet long.₄ With this I hoped to establish an approximate grade of five percent up the hill. In about two days we had this work done to what I supposed to be the summit. But it proved not to be so, although it was apparently quite as high. Early the following morning after Mr. Askey had his men in the field, we rode up the hill and I pointed out the line as far as we had gone, which ought to keep him busy for two or three weeks at least. I then set out alone to ride across that wild and mountainous country and see what I could find in the line of a feasible route. I did not make much of it as I was just out of line one way or another of where I ought to have been and it was a most long tedious trip before I got onto the second crossing of the Divide and finally into a well worn trail.

I promptly followed this until I came upon a working party following the trail in my direction and having cleared about a half mile of right-of-way. That was Mr. Lamartine's idea of locating a road — to follow a trail with all its irregularities and excesses of gradient, regardless of what improvements could be made by something of a survey. This trail branched out from a main road and I at once ordered the party to spend their time for the next two or three days in improving that road until I could find time to look the situation over. With the same instruments and a couple of men I spent the whole of the next two or three days in scouring the country leading to the Divide and seeing what I could find that would make the best route. It was during this time that I discovered Isa Lake on the Divide and adopted the canyon in which it lay as the route across the Divide. From there down I adopted the valley of Spring Creek until it entered the Firehole and followed the latter stream to where the party was in camp. I explained

17

to Mr. Wells, the foreman, the whole situation and set him to work on a new line, urging him to push the work to the utmost of his ability.

Thus, I determined the two ends of this route and by successively developing one end and then the other, I worked out the location which has been used ever since. The entire line was surveyed by myself and two men, with the hand level and a five foot stick as our sole instruments. The forest was so dense over part of the route that there was almost no way to get a view and we had to proceed a good deal in the dark. I remember I got one of my men at the top of Corkscrew Hill to climb a tree until he could get an open outlook to the east and then tie securely to the tree, where it would be distinctly visible, a large white cloth. From Shoshone Point, about three miles farther on, we found that we could actually see this cloth and it was really a good deal of help to us. When I returned to the Park seven years later, that cloth was still waving in the breeze.

With all this work completed in a manner in which I felt that things could safely proceed, I returned to Mammoth Hot Springs and gave emphatic instructions that there be no failure in getting supplies to these two parties on time. I then turned my attention to the other long stretch of road from the Thumb to the Grand Cañon which must be opened up before the circuit was complete. The work was here progressing quite vigorously at several points and it looked as though we could get the connection made clear through.

Major Jones came up about the middle of each month to pay off the force as the money was entirely in his name. It was some time in September that Captain Anderson, the Superintendent, quite unintentionally, I think, precipitated a merry little row with the Major. The Captain had just submitted his annual report. In that report he made the following reference to my connection with the road work. "Lieutenant Chittenden, U. S. Corps of Engineers, in charge of the work, is zealous, untiring, and remarkably efficient in its prosecution, and will certainly make a fine showing by the end of the year." The Major wouldn't stand for my "being in charge" and carried his complaint to Washington. It had no effect whatever except to disclose his own jealousy in the matter. I knew nothing whatever about it and the local people simply chuckled at the Major's silly discomfiture.

Later, there was a serious development in which the due part of the responsibility undoubtedly fell upon me; although my constant presence in the field should have led the office carefully to protect me. We were spending money so fast that somebody had forgotten to keep the balance sheet, and the first thing we knew we were practically at the limit of our fund. The entire working force was instantly called in and paid off and Major Jones, who was in St. Paul, was in a perfect panic and I admit, not without good reason. But his indispensable man, Lamartine, was at the

General Chittenden (left foreground) supervises
first vehicle "ascent" of Mt. Washburn

office a great deal more than I was, and the clerk himself was one of his, or Lamartine's employees. I do not know to what extent I was intentionally made a victim in the affair, or to what extent it was purely accidental. We had an immense quantity of supplies on hand and the Major in some way arranged with the dealers to carry this over to next season and save payment on them. In that way we got along, but the lesson was one I never afterward forgot. I returned to St. Paul sometime in October where I met Mrs. Chittenden and we finally located ourselves in an apartment for winter.

The next Spring, as there were no funds, of course, there was no visible prospect of any effective work until the new appropriation was available, which would not be until July. Meanwhile, one of the worst floods that ever took place in that country was raging about the middle of June. It completely wrecked a great deal of our work and my reputation as a road-builder went down as quickly as it had gone up. Mr. S. S. Huntley had just bought into the Park business and was expecting to take tourists around the new route. He and Capt. Anderson with a party quite wisely decided to pass over the route first, though I think they made a great mistake in going in a coach. They simply had an awful time. Every bridge in Spring Creek Cañon was washed out and in one place the coach sank down on its side and the water rushed up over it and came pretty nearly drowning the inmates. After a while the party returned in a state of utter discouragement. Appeals were made for me to come out and Major Jones finally consented. I took Mrs. Chittenden and our five-months-old daughter and went out. Captain Anderson had us to dinner right away and when he came to the room where Eleanor was lying on a couch she smiled very blandly at him and he remarked that that satisfied him, that a baby who could put on a smile like that was surely all right.

In the meanwhile it was a question what to do. Everybody was in ill temper and I was naturally the scapegoat. I questioned Anderson, Huntley and others most minutely as to the condition of every part of the road. From the information I received, I concluded that the case was not so desperate after all. After a careful consultation with Foreman Askey I submitted the following proposition. That if the Superintendent would advance me $500 and a certain number of enlisted men with the necessary supplies and wagons, and if the Transportation Company would contribute so much, Mr. Haynes another amount, and everybody chip in until I could get $1000 with which to pay wages, I could draw upon our surplus supplies and equip a party with which I would undertake to have the road passable within 15 days of arriving in the field. Mr. Huntley said the thing couldn't be done, but as it was the only possible chance, he consented and put up his contribution. With the utmost dispatch possible the motley party was organized and gotten into the field. I followed on my horse so as to arrive coincidently at the Upper Basin, which was to be the beginning of my 15 days. The most rigid instructions had been left that supplies must follow promptly so that there might be no complication from that cause. This requirement was not lived up to as strictly as it should have been.

I then started the parties in, assigning to some this work and to some, that; with instructions not to do a stitch of work that was not strictly necessary to making the road passable. It was surprising how rapidly we were thus able to get along. The floods were now within manageable limit, the washed out bridges were quickly replaced, and the road cleared out and made passable. I kept well ahead of the party, deciding how much work should be done at each point and thus avoiding waste of time. The average workman was so unintelligent or indifferent that I found them constantly departing from instructions through pure carelessness, and they had to be watched constantly. I taught several of them how to handle his pick and shovel in a more efficient manner and one man in particular, I taught how to chop.

We arrived at the Lake in good time but didn't find our meat there as promised and the men threatened to strike if they couldn't have it. I persuaded them to continue at least half a day. About eleven o'clock riding back to camp I heard a lot of quick sharp blows as if someone was chopping in the woods. I couldn't imagine who was there but on going over I found that it was a cook with a stick standing close by a little brook and killing the salmon as they went in pairs up over a riffle. He already had a sack full of them so that we were at least assured of fine fresh fish for dinner. Late toward evening, the promised meat came and I had no more trouble from that source. I finished the work on time as I had promised and just as I reached the Cañon, Mr. Shields and Mr. Huntley overtook me in a coach and expressed their astonishment at what I had done.

When the appropriation was available we did a good deal of work and some time in October I returned to St. Paul. The following Spring I was sent to Louisville, Kentucky. There and at my next station, Columbus, Ohio, I wrote the first edition of the *Yellowstone*.₅ My second detail at the Yellowstone was due to the urgency of Senator Carter and Mr. Huntley. General John M. Wilson, Chief of Engineers, asked me if I would like to take full charge of the Park, including the Superintendency. I replied, "No Superintendency" but that I would like to be placed in charge of the road work. I was accordingly detailed, but so particular were Senator Carter and Mr. Huntley that I should attend strictly to business, that the order as it came to me required that I stay in the Park at least four weeks on first going out. That season's work — 1899 — was the building of the new road from the Springs to Golden Gate. After I had studied out a location I took the Park authorities over it. They had to go on foot because the ground was so rough, and as we clambered through the mass of rocks which is now known as Silver Gate, they unanimously declared that it was a fine location for scenery, but impossible to build. I asked them if that was all they had to say and then proceeded to carry on the work. The location has always been a very popular one. Next year I built the Golden Gate Viaduct, which was perhaps the most difficult piece of work I executed while I was in the Park.[6]

An accomplishment which went beyond what I had ever dared to hope was the persuading of Mr. Jo Cannon to guarantee a continuing appropriation of $750,000. This enabled me to lay out the whole system, build it in quite thorough shape and place it in a condition which it has never surpassed since.

Among the more important works were the Entrance Gate at Gardiner, the concrete Melan arch over the Yellowstone River, several other fine bridges, the road through Sylvan Pass and the road over Mt. Washburn.[7] To Mr. Cannon the Park owes a debt of gratitude which it would be difficult to repay.

The work, interesting and exacting as it was, was full of troubles and disagreements. Frequently the Superintendent did not agree with me and the business management were more than once up in arms. But I always stood my ground, and although I am fully conscious of having made many mistakes, still they amount to nothing to what would have resulted had I yielded to every adverse whim or criticism.

There were, of course, very many pleasures connected with the work, the latter being of the deepest interest to me and I could readily have kept on indefinitely in such an occupation. Then there was the ever present opportunity for meeting noteworthy people and I formed many valuable friends in that way. On the whole it was a delightful detail and resulted in a definite accomplishment. It has gratified me to know that as the years go on, the appreciation of what I accomplished there has increased rather than diminished.

In 1903 I made the second revision of my book on the *Yellowstone* and later in 1915 made what will be my final revision. The result of these various re-writings was what I shall always consider a most creditable piece of work. It has taken well with the public and its sale seems to keep up in undiminished volume.[8]

* * *

Chittenden's personal contacts with Theodore Roosevelt, both as Army Engineer and as author tell an interesting story which throws light upon the characters of each man.

When Chittenden was assigned to Yellowstone National Park, President Roosevelt, who was always keenly interested in the development of the

Entrance Gate, Gardiner, dedicated by President Theodore Roosevelt, April 24, 1903

national park system, visited Yellowstone to dedicate the great Arch which had been erected at the entrance. It was a period of great stress for Chittenden. He had just received orders transferring him to the Philippines. The President's presence in the Park gave the two men a chance to get well acquainted. In his diaries Chittenden gives us an acute portrayal of those characteristics in T. R. which simultaneously endeared him to some and infuriated others.

The following excerpts are from the diary Chittenden kept from April 8 through May 3, 1903:

April 8: The President arrived today. In his general appearance and habit of speech he was not what I had anticipated, but it is evident that he is a most extra-ordinary man — more so than any other I have ever seen. I sat next to him at dinner and had a good opportunity of observing him. He left today with Billy Hofer and Major Pitcher for a walk in camp.

April 12: The President went into camp on the 9th and will remain there awhile yet. I have gotten quite well acquainted with Mr. Burroughs. Took him out to camp today. Have finished my chapter on flowers which is the last in the Yellowstone revision.

April 17, Friday: Tuesday I went into Lower Falls and stayed in camp overnight. Supped and breakfasted with the President. He was very pleasant, and did me the honor of asking me to let him see my book on the fur trade. I am in charge of the programme for laying the cornerstone of our new entrance gate on the 24th. The President is to take part.

April 19, Sunday: Friday I received orders transferring me from this work by September 1st next, and sending me to the Philippines. It is a great change, a complete reversal of duties, and on the surface looks as if it could not mean anything for my good. But I shall accept it with courage and without a word of complaint, and hope for the best. Many things of late have arisen to discourage me, and this comes as a climax. One's family counts for a great deal in such things and I don't know what mine will do; but of course, there is a way open.

April 20: It never rains but pours. Today an order came for my promotion examination. How I am to compass all I have to attend to I don't know.

April 23: Nothing new. Am studying as hard as I can but it is not easy to work under the circumstances.

May 3: Saw something of the President before leaving. He thanked me in the most profuse terms for a set of my fur trade book. On the 24th I packed up to leave the Park and at noon drove down to Gardiner to take charge of the ceremonies at the entrance gate. The President arrived at 4:00 P.M. and we all went immediately to the site of the laying where the ceremonies proceeded at once under Masonic auspices. After the laying we withdrew to an elevated platform on one part of the wall, and the President delivered an address. After the address he went to his train. I went to Mr. M. P. Carling's cabin and changed from my uniform to "cits" clothes and then went to the train, occupying Dr. Rixey's berth to Livingstone. I dined at the President's table.

A little before dinner, a Mr. Burns, President Mellen's (President of Northern Pacific R.R.) representative in the Park business, came to me (I was in Mr. Burrough's section at the time) and said, "You will not go to the Philippines". I asked him to explain and he simply repeated the statement. He then went on to say that he had been to the President and the latter had dictated in his hearing a letter to Secretary Root stating that he should regard it a calamity to remove me from that work at present, and asking to have the order rescinded.

Mr. Burroughs congratulated me, but I told him it was not a matter for congratulation, and that I should go to the President and ask him to reconsider. Presently, Mr. Burroughs and I went back to the President's car and remained alone with him for awhile on the rear platform. Then, at a signal from me, Mr. B. withdrew and I went to the Pres. and told him what I had heard, and that I felt it was not best; that it would unavoidably put me in a bad light with the (War) Department and would compel someone else to go in my place. He said that he had been so much impressed with the work I had done that he thought I ought to finish it, and asked me how long it would take. He said he would, at my request, withdraw his letter to Root, and would send a copy of it, with a personal letter, to General Gillespie direct.

There the matter stands; I feel that it is in every way (professional) better for me to go. I wrote as much to Major Abbott in the Chief's office yesterday.

On leaving the Park I went direct to St. Joseph where I held a public hearing on the 27th; and then to Kansas City where a hearing was held on the 28th; both related to the establishment of harbor lines. I addressed both meetings on the subject of the river improvements. In St. Joseph we were royally entertained by the people of the city, and in Kansas City I was the guest of the Phil Chappells.

I went to St. Louis on the night of the 28th and left there at 2:15 P.M. on the 29th, arriving in Sioux City at 10:30 A.M. on the 30th. Found everyone well.

Have finished reading the proofs of "Yellowstone". The LaBarge book will appear right away. The home people here, and in fact, everyone, have expressed the greatest regret at my being transferred to other duty.

In the Park I saw something of the President. He is certainly a man of great force and ability. He is in perfect health. His appetite is strong. The teeth that figure so in caricature are the most perfect I have ever seen. His range of knowledge is wide and he uses Latin quotations in his conversation as freely as a lawyer in his legal work. He never talks easily but always in a strenuous manner as if forcing out and biting off all he says. He is very particular about formalities but likes to have them very simple. He gave explicit instructions about the ceremonies at Gardiner and in particular wanted me so to arrange it that the people would crowd in close to his stand. He said that to have fifty feet of empty space between him and his hearers robbed him of all his power over an audience. I suppose his near sight has something to do with it.

He is very impetuous and hasty, and but for his clear vision and sane, single-minded view of things, would get into difficulty often. I saw an instance in my own case. Upon my recommendation, the people of Gardiner had appealed to the Secretary of the Interior to take water from the Gardiner River within the Park. It was a necessary case for they could not get it elsewhere. The Secretary of the Interior denied their request. They asked me to see the President. The day before the President left he and Pitcher rode over to my office and the President thanked me for my book. I then told him about the Gardiner matter. It aroused him to a considerable temper and he said with much vehemence and a forcible gesture, "You give my compliments to the Secretary of the Interior and tell him that I desire him to grant the request of these people." He repeated his command with increasing energy at last twice. I did not know what to do for it seemed an extraordinary proceeding for me to write to the Secretary. But I drew up a letter as directed, but held it to show to Secretary Loeb before it went. Fortunately the President reconsidered his actions next day and said he would write himself. In his address at Gardiner he referred to the matter and laughingly told the people of Gardiner that "Captain Chittenden and I have fixed these matters up to your satisfaction."

In like manner it seemed to me that this action in regard to my Philippine orders was hasty.

On the day of the ceremonies of laying the cornerstone of the Arch, I received a telegram signed "All of us", from my Helena friends, which read: "We congratulate the country on the hand that built the Arch".

May 5: Routine work all day. No news.

May 19: On May 12 I held a final meeting in the Kansas City Harbor Line case. I returned to Sioux City on the 13th and remained there until Thursday night the 14th when I left for the Park via St. Paul. (I forgot to say that on the 11th I visited Ft. Leavenworth). Reached the Park today and found things moving in fairly good shape. No news yet from Washington in regard to my going to the Philippines.

May 25, Monday: Thursday I drove out to Appolinaris Spring and back. It was cold and snowy and the ground was covered with snow. Saturday I drove to the (?) Camp on the northern slope of Mt. Washburn and came back yesterday.

June 14. On June 1st I went out to the Canon to look at the work there. Came in next day and found telegrams requiring my presence at Kansas City on account of the great flood. Left that afternoon and reached Kansas City Friday P.M. having to go via St. Louis. The Flood was certainly a terrible visitation to the towns from Kansas City and up the river. It would scarcely be possible to exaggerate this.

I left K.C. Saturday night and reached home 6:00 P.M. Sunday. Left there Wednesday night via St. Paul and reached here (Yellowstone Park) yesterday.

My Yellowstone book (revised) is out; also my book on History Missouri River Navigation.

My order to the Philippines has been revoked. News came to me in these terms: "Orders will issue in two days revoking your orders to the Philippines against your protest". My efforts to prevent the order being revoked were evidently effective, but President Mellen of the Northern Pacific saw President Roosevelt in Oregon and got the president to countermand [the] order positively.

Have accepted a proposition to write a book on Mississippi River Navigation.

⋆　　⋆　　⋆

See Footnotes₄ in Appendix to Chapter III, Journals of Western Trips for an account of a later clash between President Roosevelt and Chittenden. Each man, devoted to his own concept of the proper techniques of conservation, collided in full view of the nation.

III

Journals of Western Trips

Editor's Notes

Much of the material which went into the writing of *The American Fur Trade of the Far West* was gathered on these trips to Wyoming, Colorado, Idaho and the Pacific Coast. In several instances, Chittenden's observations in these journals are almost identical with passages in his fur trade history. The author surveyed Independence Rock, traced a portion of the route of the Astorians, and followed an occasional stretch of the Oregon Trail.

Deeply moved by his first glimpse of the great Trail, Chittenden wrote: "Romance and tragedy are written in every mile, and the deep and abiding impression which this pilgrimage made along this surface of the earth is but a symbol of the deeper and more lasting impression which it wrought upon the life of the nation".

In August 1897 he combined his surveys with visits to old Fort Laramie and other sites where his imagination summoned up the ghosts of Jim Bridger, Ashley, Sublette and other giants of the fur trade. The great story is beginning to ferment in his mind.

The western trips which Chittenden reports in his journals resulted from work assigned while he was serving as Secretary of the Missouri River Commission. He personally visited many sections of the West, reporting on numerous reservoir sites, finally submitting an exhaustive report which was printed by Congress as House Document 141, 56th Congress, 2nd Session, largely reprinted in the *Congressional Record*. The report enthusiastically advocated government aid in irrigation work, at least to the extent of storing water. The report became very popular throughout the West, and a potent factor in alerting Congress to the necessity of taking action.

Journal of a Trip to the Pacific Coast, December 1896

December 9, 1896

Left St. Louis at 9 a.m. in company with Mr. Blaisdell who was on his way to the Osage River to visit the government work at Lock No. 1.₁ At Chamois we met Asst. Engineer Fox for a moment at the station. Mr. Blaisdell got off at Osage City. Reached Kansas City at 6:30 p.m. and left at 7:30 p.m. Talked politics in smoking room 'till 10 p.m. with three gentlemen none of whom I knew. The net conclusion arrived at was that if it is a fact that the value of gold has appreciated and that the fall of prices is due to this cause, then there is something in the silver agitation, if not, not.₂

December 10, 1896

When I woke up we were well out on the prairies. It was a beautiful morning and the familiar site of the vast plains was very pleasing. I caught a first glimpse of the mountains — Pikes Peak — about 11 a. m. — some distance East of Hugo station. We reached Dunn at 2:10 p.m. After dinner, I visited Denver and called on Mr. Sumner, State Engineer. I very unexpectedly met Lieut. Byram of the Army who is now on duty with the State Militia. After leaving the State House, I visited the libraries to see if I could find a certain work I had intended to bring with me, but had left behind. After supper, I called on Mrs. Mattie Powers, my former pupil in Cuba, New York.₃

December 11, 1896

Rose at 7 a.m. After breakfast called at Santa Fe offices to see about trains. Then went to Jackson's photo gallery to get some points about taking photographs of scenery in mountainous country. Made appointment to meet photographer in pm with instrument. Then went to Capitol and met Mr. Sumner and several other engineers and looked up the matter of reservoir sites. At noon called on Mr. Hale and spent half an hour with him. In pm took instrument to Jackson's and obtained instructions as to handling it.

At about 3 pm I went to meeting of American Society of Irrigation Engineers and listened to discussion. After adjournment I met several gentlemen connected with the Society and had considerable discussion with them. The general drift of opinion among these engineers was that it was impossible to get the government to do anything and that the lands should be given to the States.[4]

In the evening I met Mr. Ellwood Mead of Wyoming and had considerable talk with him on the subject of my trip. At 8:45 I left via the Santa Fe for Denver. The train stopping at Colorado Springs for the night, I went to a small place near the station where transients are kept and stayed overnight.

December 12, 1896

Got my breakfast at the above place and left on train at 6:30 am. A beautiful sight presented itself just as we were leaving Colorado Springs. It was still quite dark, the twilight not having sensibly diminished the obscurity of night. But the rays of the sun had already touched the summit of Pike's Peak and covered it with a crimson color. At the same time a brilliant star was just about to set behind the peak but hung for a time exactly over the summit like a great electric light. It was a beautiful and striking sight. It was 10:00 pm when we reached Larny Junction where the branch road leaves for Santa Fe. There were many interesting sights both in scenery and in the peculiar customs of the people and Indians as we approached New Mexico. The Spanish peaks stood out in great prominence. I had seen them from the other side in 1890. Reached Santa Fe and was installed at the Palace Hotel at about midnight.

December 13, 1896

The next morning I took my photographic apparatus and went about town to get some views. I first went to the summit of the hill where old Fort Marcy stands. I took six pictures there of the city and mountains, and then went to the cathedral, San Miguel church, and the Plaza and took two pictures of each. My day was most interestingly spent. I met a Mr. Raynes and wife of Boston — she a Spanish lady of noble descent, and a most original character. It was a great novelty and pleasure to be entertained by her. In the afternoon we went to the Plaza and listened to music by an Indian band and saw the heterogeneous mixture of Indian, Mexican, and American in the crowd that gathers there of a Sunday afternoon. I walked for a considerable time through the streets of this quaint and ancient town and experienced feelings not unlike those which the antiquities of Italy inspired when I visited that country. I left at 9:30 pm for Phoenix, Ariz.

December 14, 1896

All day on the train. I met a good many people mostly bound for Phoenix and had a very enjoyable trip. The scenery was generally mountainous, but became much less so near the end of the day's journey in the neighborhood of the San Francisco mountains. The trip from Ash Fork to Phoenix was made by night and without a sleeper. It was a wretched experience. I forgot to mention the forming of an acquaintance on the train on the 12th, of a mining promoter, or speculator in mining properties. My experiences with him are written out in another place.

December 15, 16, 17, 1896

Reached Phoenix at 7 am and have since been in attendance at the Irrigation Congress. Have met numbers of people, some very interesting ones. Among them are ex-Gov. Trilte of Arizona Territory, Mr. F. H. Newell of the U.S.G.S., Judge Best, Asst. U.S. Land Commissioner, Mr. J. D. Schuyler, distinguished Irrigation Engineer, and Mr. Wright, author of the celebrated Wright law. The Congress has been of great value to me in making me better acquainted with the views of the Western people, but a great disappointment in the misused prevalence of a spirit of impracticable method in trying to enlist government aid. It seems that every advocate of government aid wants to provide a possible job for himself. So an important enterprise, vital to the interests of these people, will fail, largely through the fault of the people themselves.

On the evening of the 16th some Prince Indian students and children gave an exhibition on the stage of the Congress Hall. They were from the Indian school here.

I forgot to say that Capt. Palfrey, late of the Corps of Engineers, but now retired, is here as a delegate.

December 18, 1896

Today was spent most enjoyably in a trip to the head of the Arizona Canal and then back along the Consolidated Canal Company's line. We passed on our way out several orange and olive groves and plucked and ate ripe oranges. We passed through acres and acres of the giant cactus which made a remarkable impression on the landscape. There were also many other varieties of cactus of remarkable and luxuriant growth. The mountain scenery was exceptionally fine. The division dam of the Arizona Land Company extends obliquely across the stream, and develops a crest of perhaps 1500 feet. This is of much importance in taking care of the floods. In the afternoon we travelled down the left bank of the Salt River, visited the head gate of Dr. Chandler's ditch — a very well-built work — and then visited a large dredge at work on the ditch, and power plant farther down involving some novel features. The Doctor lets the water from off a bluff to the level of the river bottom. He has a head of something like 50 feet which he utilizes in producing electricity. This is to be conveyed up the valley to a point where wells can be found with water only 20 feet or less below the surface of the canal. With the fall of 50 ft. and lift of 20 it is expected to pump water enough to run the power plant, thus producing perpetual motion without resort to a running stream.

After leaving the power plant we drove to Dr. Chandler's house and partook of an excellent lunch, after which we took a train to Phoenix, arriving about 7:30 pm.

Saturday, December 19, 1896

Left at 7 am for California. There were also on board Mr. and Mrs. Schuyler, Mr. C. C. Wright, Mr. Maxwell of San Francisco, and several others from California. The day passed off pleasantly and resulted in obtaining considerable information. In places the scenery en route was particularly fine, especially at the great Amphitheater not far South of Ash Fork. The engineering work at this point is quite equal to any I have seen in Colorado.

Sunday, December 20, 1896

Today was spent en route to Los Angeles and San Diego. I had considerable conversation with Messrs. Wright, Maxwell, and Schuyler about the workings of the Wright law. From their conversation I learned something of the good and bad points of the law. Mr. Schuyler and I arranged a programme for my trip through Southern California. At Los Angeles I bade my acquaintances good-bye, and after having bought my ticket, unexpectedly met Mr. Nelson Patrick, of Omaha, with his private car, and a party bound for San Diego. They insisted on my riding with them, which I did, and passed a very pleasant afternoon. I reached San Diego and went on to National City, three or four miles beyond, reaching there soon after 6 pm.

After supper I looked up Mr. Savage, to whom I had previously sent Mr. Schuyler's letter of introduction, and spent the evening with him, looking over his photographs.

Monday, December 21, 1896

At about 10 am we set out for the Sweetwater Dam, reaching there about noon. We spent two hours looking at this interesting work, of which full descriptions have been written.

The Golden Gate Viaduct

At 2:30 pm we set out for the [   ] Dam arriving there just before sunset. This novel piece of work presents one point of great interest to engineers. It is a rock fill dam, but has the additional feature of a steel core ¼ inch thick supported by 1 ft. of concrete on each side. If the settling of the dam does not rupture the plate, nor rub off the protecting concrete so as to expose the plate to corrosion, the scheme ought to work well. The rock in the fill was stated to have cost in place less than 50 cents per cu. yd.

We ate supper at the dam and waited for moon rise to start home. The distance was 15 miles and we covered it at 9:30 pm. It was somewhat chilly but very pleasant.

Tuesday, December 22, 1896

Set out at 6:30 am to visit the La Mesa dam. The peculiarity of construction of this dam was the use of the hydraulic process by which the materials were washed down a slope on to the dam and allowed to settle there gradually building the dam up. In this particular case the work, for an earthen dam, was expensive, the conditions for the use of the hydraulic process being unfavorable.

On our return from the dam we passed through the city of San Diego and had a good opportunity to see that interesting town.

At 12:30 pm I left National City for Escondido, reaching the latter place at 6:30 pm. Met Mr. Tabor at the hotel, to whom I had sent a letter of introduction. We spent the evening looking at photos of the works, and talking over the general subject of irrigation.

Wednesday, December 23, 1896

Set out at an early hour and drove to the Escondido dam distant 8 miles. The drive was particularly fine, much of the road being a steep grade along the mountain side, affording many fine views. The Escondido dam is the simplest type of rock fill in which many pains are taken to make it impervious to water. The up stream slope is faced with a plank sheeting, of which I have placed a description in my notes. On our return to town, we drove through some of the orchards of the district and had a good opportunity to see a variety of distributing methods. I should have stated that both at San Diego and here pipes are largely used so that one has frequently no more visible evidence of the course of the water than in the water system of a city. The use of wooden pipes, and the skill used in their construction, were a good deal of a surprise to me.

At 12:30 pm. I set out with a conveyance and drove to Oceanside where I took a train for Riverside reaching the latter place at 7:30 pm.

Here I found Mr. Newman, an engineer of Swedish descent, and of long experience in California irrigation, waiting for me. We spent the evening together in a general discussion of subjects pertaining to the object of my visit.

Thursday, December 24, 1896

Spent most of the forenoon in riding about Riverside with Mr. Newman and in examining the canals, distributing gates, flumes, and magnificent grounds and avenues. It was the most perfect product of the art of irrigation that I had yet seen although I understand that Redlands and Highland surpass it.

The cement lined canals looked exceedingly fine and I was astonished to find that some of the more recent are found of only half an inch thickness of cement. Before putting it on the sandy sides of the trench they are sprayed with water until they pack well. Then they are packed again, sprayed rapidly under heavy water pressure so as to pit and roughen the surface. When the cement is put on it seems to solidify the sand backing also to a depth of two or three inches. The work seems to stand about as well as that composed of stone and cement, constructed previously and its cost is only $3000 per mile as against $10,000 for the other.

At noon I left Riverside for Hemet arriving at the latter place at about 2:30 pm. There I met Mr. Schuyler, Prof. Moses of the Cal. State University, and Col. Mayberry, the general manager, and part owner, of the Hemet Land District. At about 4 pm. the Colonel took Prof. Moses and myself for a ride over his property and we must have travelled seven or eight miles. We inspected his ditch system, saw and examined their potato digging machines. The capacity of these machines is very great and the potato yield in this section was over 100 bushels per acre and two crops at that.

That evening we spent in very pleasant chat in the Hotel parlor. The hotel was splendidly appointed considering its location, and the cooking surpassed anything that I had yet seen on my trip.

Friday, December 25, 1896

Christmas Day spent in a ride to the Hemet Dam (23) miles and back. We started at 7 am but as the road was up hill nearly all the way, and very steep in places, and as we stopped at several points to inspect the flumes and similar works, it was after noon before we reached the dam. I was particularly struck with the perfect construction of the flumes. They were about 30 inches wide and 15 inches deep and made only of ordinary lumber. But it was very rare that we could find a leak. The bottom boards were fixed with caulking joints. In the angles between the sides and bottom a three-cornered piece was placed and then everything filled with pitch. The success of its construction was certainly remarkable, and at the same time cheap. Provision was made for an additional side board which involved an ingenious arrangement.

By cutting an offset in the post the upper plank can be slipped down a little behind the lower and a three-cornered piece put on as at the bottom.

We spent nearly three hours at the dam and looked over that splendid structure very completely. I was astonished at being told that its cost was less than $3.50 per cu. yd. The figures I have in my notes.

I should have mentioned an incident that occurred on our way up. The Colonel tried to call my attention to everything of interest, and when nearly at the top of the hill he stopped his team (he and Prof. Moses were together and Mr. Schuyler and I were behind in our own conveyance) until we caught up. Then he said, "Captain, do you see those acorns", I, thinking that I would of course see them at once, nodded assent, and commenced looking very hard to find them. But not an oak tree nor an acorn could I see, and was a good deal embarrassed in consequence. After we started ahead again, I told Mr. Schuyler of my predicament, and he then pointed out the acorns to me in the trunk of a pine tree. The woodpeckers had picked it full of holes and into these had put acorns, one in each hole, and the fit was so perfect that I was unable to pull any of them out. Some of these immense trunks were filled with acorns, and there must have been thousands and thousands of them in a single tree. Mr. S. stated that they were put there by the woodpeckers themselves, but some one else said that the holes were bored for worms and squirrels took advantage of them.[5]

Our ride down the mountain that afternoon was exhilarating in the extreme. For six miles down the "grade", as it is called, the road hangs on the side of the cliff and contains the most remarkable series of windings and curves that I ever saw. Down this grade we sped at the rate of 12 miles an hour, and nothing but good driving saved us from destruction. But as we had good drivers (Col. M. and Mr. S.) the experience was most enjoyable and one not to be forgotten.

We reached home at 10 minutes of 6 pm having made the 23 miles since 3:10 pm. We then sat down to a Christmas dinner which lacked only the presence of home friends to make most enjoyable.

This irrigation enterprise at Hemet appeared to me to rest on the best financial basis of any I had seen. The works were constructed with marvelous economy, they are ample for forthcoming requirements for many years to come, the land to be irrigated is of unsurpassed quality.

Saturday, December 26, 1896

Left Hemet at 6:46 am. for Los Angeles arriving at the latter place at noon. On our way we stopped at Orange for 50 minutes and took a drive around that little town. Immediately after reaching Los Angeles we went to the place where the harbor commission was sitting to determine whether the government should improve Santa Monica or San Pedro as the port of Los Angeles. The fight is really between the people of California and Mr. Huntington of the Southern Pacific, with nature favoring the people. Much doubt is entertained as to the outcome owing to the influence of Huntington but the board certainly *looked* like an intelligent, honest set of men and money may not control them.[6]

At one o'clock we sat down to an elegant dinner at Mr. Schuyler's home, which was again incomplete from the absence of home friends.

In the afternoon I visited several photographers and ordered pictures of the works I had visited. I also called upon Mr. Wright who gave me a letter to an acquaintance of his at Modesto whither I was going. At nine pm I left for Modesto. The car was stifling hot, and in my effort to get some air I caught a severe cold in my throat.

Sunday, December 27, 1896

Reached Modesto at noon, and started at once for the La Grange dam distant 33 miles. We made the distance by 4:30 pm. We walked from La Grange village to the dam, a mile and a half, and I got much overheated.

Monday, December 28, 1896

Stayed that night at La Grange, and left at 6:30 am. for Modesto arriving at 10 am. There I made arrangements for photos of work and obtained some other information. Left Modesto at noon and reached San Francisco at 5 pm. My cold is much worse and worries me a good deal. Here may be a proper place for a few comments on the operation of the Wright law.

I found almost universal dissatisfaction with it and yet a very general faith that it would ultimately work well. It is in fact hard to conceive of a plan by which the general community or portions thereof, can take up the subject of irrigation without using the principle which lies at the bottom of the Wright law. The great difficulty I found to be injudicious and ill advised action at first. Contrary to law, where bonds failed to sell, they were turned in in payment for work at prices which made the work cost the districts more than twice what it ought to. Thus the Tuolomne (La

Grange) dam cost over $13 per cu. yd., the Hemet less than $3.50 and the latter was at a less accessible point. It generally happened that the boards of directors were not made up of practical business men, but of farmers or others who knew little either of finance or engineering. They thus fell the victims of schemes and in many instances their bonds were disposed of, the debt saddled on the district, and yet the works were not completed and the district was without water. Such a condition, of course, caused wide-spread discontent and will continue to do so, for the way out of the difficulty is not easy to see. It is suggested by some that none but the owners of land capable of being irrigated should comprise the voting population of the district on irrigation matters. Now village property within the limits of the district is taxed and manhood suffrage holds as in other elections. Probably with the above qualifications no district could be found, and much of the business talent would be excluded if it should be. Another suggestion is that there should be somebody, as a State Board of Control, whose duty should be to pass upon all propositions to organize districts, to examine the practicability of the project, and otherwise to supervise the carrying of it out. Some such check seems absolutely necessary to prevent precipitate and ill-advised actions. It is probable that the law will stand, but it will have a hard fight for existence.

Tuesday, December 29, 1896

Spent day in city. Lunched with Mr. Maxwell at club. Called at Mrs. Victor's but did not find her in. Spent an hour with Col. Suter. Secured transportation requests for my return home, and looked up the matter of some purchases. My cold is worse today and gives me much anxiety. Shall start home tomorrow.

Wednesday, December 30, 1896

Spent all day in San Francisco, but so much dispirited on account of my sickness that I was not able to do much. Called upon Major Davis of my Corps and at noon received a call from Mrs. Frances Fuller Victor which lasted for about three hours and would have been very enjoyable had I not been so indisposed. I left San Francisco for the East at 6 pm.

Thursday, December 31, 1896

On train en route for Salt Lake City — suffering greatly with my cold.

Friday, January 1, 1897

Reached Salt Lake City about 8 am. Remained about the hotel all day and finally concluded to go to a hospital until in better condition. Went to St. Mark's hospital that morning and remained there until Tuesday pm.

January 5. Left for Cheyenne on the evening train.

Wednesday, January 6, 1897

At Laramie Mr. Nellis Anthiel, an old classmate of mine at Ten Broek Academy met and accompanied me to Cheyenne. We had a pleasant talk over old times. At Cheyenne I visited the capitol and looked over maps of reservoir sites — practically settling upon one.

Thursday, January 7, 1897

At 2 am. left Cheyenne for St. Louis travelling all day. Reached Omaha at 4:45 pm.

Friday January 8, 1897

Reached St. Louis at 7 am still suffering from my cold but able to be about and not looking so badly as might have been expected from my illness.

Chittenden Road, Mt. Washburn

Journal of a Trip to Wyoming and Colorado, May 1897

April 20, 1897

Left St. Louis via Wabash for Omaha at 9 pm.

May 1, 1897

Arrived in Council Bluffs at 11:10 am. Visited government works and spent afternoon there with Mr. Lange, Asst. Engr. Paid off force. At 6 pm. went to Omaha and called on Mr. F. M. Richardson and family in evening.

May 2, 1897

Left Omaha via U.P. at 8:20 a.m. A pleasant, but very dusty ride to Cheyenne, where I arrived at 10:30 pm. Noted more particularly than ever before the extreme shallowness of the bed of the Platte below its banks. On the South Fork it seemed by 2 or 3 feet below the top of the bank, though nearly half a mile wide. The bed has built itself up slightly in places and the immediate bank appears higher than the lands a short distance back. The two forks, as is well known, approach each other for many miles at a very acute angle. It is a flat plain between them from the junction for a distance of about 19 miles; the bluff between beginning to rise from the plain a little below Sutherland on the U.P.R.R.

Cheyenne, May 3, 1897

Rose early and after breakfast took a stroll of an hour around the outskirts of town looking at the mountains and prairies. The mountains appear to be heavily covered with snow and form, as always, a beautiful sight. At 9 am. I went to Mr. Mead's office — State Engineer — and was with him two hours. We talked over the whole matter of reservoirs, irrigation, the land question, grazing and sheep industry, etc. I was much impressed with Mr. Mead's views on the land question and he undoubtedly sees it pretty nearly in its true light. Although I should not want to see the public lands turned over absolutely to the States, still it is only just that some law shall be passed which will make the nomadic industries bear their proportion of the public administration.

I was agreeably surprised to find Mr. Mead on the whole favorably disposed toward the project which I am engaged on and it is not impossible that something may yet come of it.

At about 11 am Mr. Mead presented me to Gov. Richards with whom I had a pleasant chat. I then went to the hotel for dinner and at 1:30 pm Mr. Mead called on me and we had considerable further conversation. He introduced me to Mr. Butterick, Secy. of State, a very pleasant man of fine presence, and to Judge [   ]. At 2:45 pm I left for Denver, Judge [   ] being on the train. We talked a good deal about written matters. Passed through a fine irrigated belt near [   ]. Saw the ruins of old Fort [   ]. Sky too heavy to get best effect of mountains. Reached Denver at 6 pm. At 8 pm called on Hale and family and had some further talk about reservoirs, etc.

Tuesday, May 4, 1897

At 9 am called on Hale and made arrangements to see parties later in day. I then went to State house where I met State Engineer Field and ex-State Engineer Sumner. Looked over maps of reservoir sites. Then went with Sumner to see Mr. Allen, Chief Engineer of Water Company and made appointment with him to meet Mr. Cheesman, president of company in pm. On returning to hotel found Capt. Berthaud of Golden waiting for me. He remained till 2 pm. Made me a present of a very valuable book by Hayden which I had never seen before. He also gave me considerable information of an historical character. At 2 pm went to State House and called on Gov. Adams. At 3 pm went with Messrs. Sumner and Allen to call on Mr. Cheesman. We discussed the matter of this water company's rights in the Platte reservoir site on Goose Creek. Mr. Cheesman seemed very desirous that the government should commence the work of reservoir construction, but, as might have been expected, would not wish to *give* away any valuable rights to the site in question.

At 4 pm called on Mr. Hufe in company with Mr. Hale. Mr. Hufe is Engineer of another company which expects to operate up the valley.

At 6:30 pm went to dinner at Mr. Hale's house. Returned at 8:30 pm and met Messrs. Sumner and Hufe with whom I spent balance of evening.

In afternoon telegraphed Maltby to come on with party, and in course of evening received word that he would start that night.

May 5, 1897

Left Denver at 8:15 am in company with Mr. Hufe for Platte reservoir site. Arrived at South Platte at 9:30 am. Took stage and reached Turnbull soon after noon. Kept on with stage to Amos Ranch 1½ miles, and hired separate conveyance for balance of distance, 8 miles. Route over mountains very steep. On top of ridge encountered a thunder shower. Reached site of reservoir dam about 4:30 pm, and after examining it carefully, left at 5:15 pm. Returned to Amos' Ranch at 8 pm, stayed there for supper and then walked to Turnbull where we put up for night. The section of country through which we travelled was extremely interesting from a scenic point of view, but was pervaded with the gloom of business decadence. The Platte valley had recently witnessed a great boom, towns had sprung up, and lots had been sold. But the "supposed finds" did not develop and the whole population had left except a few indigent hangers on, lazy and shiftless beyond conception. They would sit together on the steps of some deserted store and mourn the timidity of capital in not seeking so promising a field. They all said that even a common prospector with no other capital than his pick, shovel and pan could make $2.00 per day. I wondered why some of them did not go at it.

Mr. Amos was one of the meekest and most inoffensive individuals, in appearance, that I ever saw. When asked what I owed him, he stood abashed and silent for fully two minutes and then said $4.50. The distance driven was 8 miles and back, and the team utterly worthless for quick driving.

May 6, 1897

Remained at Turnbull all night in a most questionable bed, and ate there meals of even more questionable food. In forenoon walked up Platte nearly 3 miles and enjoyed it much. Day almost perfect and air clear and invigorating. Had considerable talk with the shiftless inhabitants of this quondam city. At 1 pm left on stage for Platte city where we took train for Denver. Met Maltby and party on return and spent evening in arranging details of work.

May 7, 1897

Spent day in Denver completing arrangements for work. Saw Capt. Palfry and called at his house. Called on Gen. Wheaton who was to retire next day. Had considerable talk with various parties. Left at 6 pm for Laramie. Stopped at Cheyenne at 10:30 and stayed overnight.

May 8, 1897

Left Cheyenne at 7:45 am for Laramie where I arrived at 10:20 am.

Saw Nellis Antheil an old classmate at Franklinville. Took dinner with him and was a good deal alarmed at the fact that the whole family of children were only just recovering from measles — I have never had this disease. Saw city engineer and looked over reservoir drawings. Took a ride in afternoon to site a few miles West of town. Visited University on my return to get data. Met three of the professors. Spent evening at Antheil's and met a young lady who had been at the Yellowstone the previous summer.

May 9, 1897

Left at 8 am for Wood's Landing, distant nearly 30 miles up the Laramie, to visit reservoir site, and city engineer went along. Returned at 6 pm. Dined at Mr. Buck's and Antheil's folks and Mr. and Mrs. Jackson were present. Left at midnight for Rawlins. Arrived in Rawlins at 4:20 am. Left on stage for Devils Gate on Sweetwater at 7:30 am. Ride cold and unpleasant and greater part of country extremely uninviting. At one point crossed a ridge just above what is called Brown's Cañon. It is a striking bit of scenery and a noted place for winds. That the stories of severe gales that blow over this point are not exaggerated appears from the growth of sagebrush along the ridge. It all lies nearly horizontal as if pulled over with a rope, and the ground is blown away around the stalks leaving only little mounds of earth. It is said to be unsafe to pass this point in time of gales with covered vehicles for they will be overturned. My driver said that even with his open wagon the rear wheels would be blown around at a considerable angle with the road making a sort of side-wise travel. I was also told by Mr. Bothwell, whom I met next day, that on January 4 he and Mrs. B. were going to Rawlins and encountered a heavy gale while crossing this ridge. It was impossible to make the horses move against it and he had to get out of the wagon and lead and drive them from the ground. The wind was so terrific however, that Mrs. B could not keep the robes around her and it was actually necessary to lash both her and them to the wagon, although the latter was in imminent danger of upsetting. The ascent of the ridge, which consumed considerable time completely exhausted Mrs. B. Stern Ranch where we took dinner was a dismal place beyond description. Even more dismal and utterly repulsive, was the dinner provided for travellers. I tried in vain to eat, but was charged 50 cents as if I had partaken of a good repast.

From Stern Ranch we crossed the sand hills, a most difficult stretch of road. It was 5 pm when we reached Ferris. From there the stage man varied his route somewhat to take me nearer to Devil's Gate. He left me about 2 miles from Tom Sun's ranch. It was already dark, but there was a good moon and I walked the distance in a short time. Had supper at the ranch and went to bed at 10 pm.

May 11, 1897

Rose at 7 am having slept soundly for 9 hours. My loss of rest the night before and over 130 miles of wagon travel the previous two days made me very tired. In the morning I went with Mr. Sun to visit the Gate and get some views. It is a very interesting and remarkable formation and a perfect site for a reservoir dam. The view from the summit of this rocky ridge entirely satisfied me that it is the locality mentioned by Irving as having been passed by the Astorians Oct. 28, 1812.[1] I could not wonder that they stopped to repose and feast for one day when they came to the beautiful valley above this spot, for a more delightful scene I have not often witnessed. As a landview it was not dissimilar to the view of the Hudson from West Point, for the broad expanse of plain both above and below the Gate was like a vast rim surrounded by rugged and broken mountains. Below the Gate, 7 miles distant was Independence Rock, rising like an island from the plain. In early days these plains must have been great resorts for buffalo, as indeed the Astorians found them. Returned to the Ranch at 11 am and went to the trout pond for half an hour to fish, but without success, the water being too high. After dinner Mr. Sun went with me to Independence Rock where I spent two hours looking over this singular and historic natural feature. I walked entirely around it and climbed to the top. I saw many old names, but none as ancient as I had hoped. The weather evidently wears even granite very rapidly. It is quite possible, however, that a close scrutiny might discover some interesting relics, but as the Rock is upwards of three quarters of a mile around, and covers, probably 15 acres, it was impossible to examine it closely in the time at my disposal.

At 3:30 pm I set out on horseback for the ranch of Albert J. Bothwell, 8 miles below. At this place I was treated to one of the pleasantest surprises I have ever met. I found as delightful a family as one could meet in any city. Mr. B. is an exceptionally shrewd business man and at the same time a very excellent scholar, his particular studies being in the line of geology and evolution. For the great teachers, Spencer, Huxley, Darwin, and Tyndall, he has an admiration amounting almost to worship. He has a remarkably well equipped library and is a most interesting conversationalist.

Mrs. B. likewise, is a good scholar, something of an author, and a most estimable and entertaining lady. Mr. B. is her second husband, and her two children, 16 and 12 years, are by her former husband whose name was Church.

There was also living with them a lady by the name of Wadsworth who was like the other denizens of this delightful spot — engaging and hospitable to the utmost degree.

Mr. B. has built up an extensive ranch in the very lower part of the beautiful Sweetwater Valley. He farms out portions of his ranch to small farmers, but finds great difficulty in securing competent men. He has a large amount of ditches on his lands and take it all in all seemed to me to be very well "fixed".

I found on my arrival at this place that it would be impossible for me to visit the Platte Cañon and get to Bessemer (on the road to Casper) the next day. So I concluded to defer my home trip one day and spend the next night also on this ranch.

I forgot to say that I found Loren Sun a most entertaining old gentleman, full of reminscences of early times, and a hospitable host. He has an interesting family and I enjoyed my short stay there very much.

May 12, 1897

At 9 am Mr. B. and I set out on horseback for the Platte Cañon, distance over 12 miles. Most of the way was over sage brush plains, and the way that Mr. B. took us through those clusters of tough growth rather alarmed me for the safety of the riders. But the horses picked their way at a rapid gallop for mile after mile with scarce a stumble. We arrived at the Cañon at half past 10 and I found a sight that would have done credit to the Yellowstone Park. The cañon appeared to me to be from 700 to 1000 feet deep — too deep to be photographed from the top. I therefore at once started down a narrow chasm and by dint of severe work got down some 500 feet where I had a good view both up and down. At this point there is a rectangular bend in the river and I was exactly in its angle. I secured several exposures. The return climb was fatiguing in the extreme, and I was compelled to pause every little while to rest. The whole trip in and out consumed an hour and a half.

This spot is, without doubt, the fiery narrows of the returning Astorians. The place is most interesting geologically. The primary rocks, a reddish granite, compose the lower half of the Cañon walls and upon these, with a dip to the N. E. of some 20 degrees, are the rocks of successive ages, all exposed in a distance of a few miles. The red of the sand stones formed a striking feature of the landscape.

At 1 pm we set out to return. On the way I was struck with the great beauty of the prairie flowers which carpeted the ground with the most beautiful variety of colors.

We reached the ranch at 4 pm and the rest of the day was spent most enjoyably in conversation and discussion. Mr. B. and I spent several hours over the various features of evolutionary science, and had quite a sharp contest over the value of Genesis, as a scientific account of creation.

In the evening the ladies sang and performed on the piano. At 10 pm, I retired.

[May 13, 1897]

The morning was spent very pleasantly at the Bothwell Ranch in various discussions of mutual interest. Lunch was served at 10:30 am in order that Mr. B. might take me to Berthaton to catch the stage for Casper. I took pictures of the ranch and of Mr. B.'s division dam on the Sweetwater. We arrived at Berthaton at 12 noon but had to wait until 1:30 pm for the stage. Mr. B. remained with me until its arrival when I bade him goodbye after a most delightful sojourn with him and his family.

The driver of the stage was a Mr. Merrill, one of the most constant talkers I ever saw. But the range of his conversation was as limited as his verbosity was abundant. Two topics only formed the burden of his talk during the 8 hours which it took us to make the 54 miles to Casper. One was stage-driving and I was graciously let into the mysteries of that difficult business and had pointed out to me the many little points which combine to make it successful. His own history in the business was also related, and every now and then he would ask, after perpetrating some fancied pleasantry—"Pretty good joke wasn't it," to which I invariably replied, "yes".

The other topic which filled his mind was the hoped-for extension of the new RR and an anxiety to have some hint of where the town, which would probably spring up in this neighborhood, would most likely be located. He couldn't get rid of the idea that I was an advance agent of the new RR and could give him hints of great importance. After several denials, I finally humored his fancy and he became very much enthused. He was sure that if I would give him a little inside information, he could enable me to secure land cheaper than I as a stranger could get it myself. Etc. Etc.

But what attracted my attention most of all on this long ride, was the presence, almost all the way, of the great Oregon Trail. There was a deep and suggestive meaning in that now deserted furrow that gave me much to think of and relieved the monotony of the ride. The trail was scarcely ever less than 100 feet wide and frequently covered a breadth of 200 feet. Sometimes it was but a faint impression on the prairie, at others (and generally), it lay about 2 feet below the surrounding ground, while occasionally the later action of the winds had scoured it out to the depth of 6 feet. Over long distances this trail will continue visible for centuries to come, unless, indeed, it is obliterated by agriculture. It is a worthy monument to the mighty movement by which it was produced. It is lined with the graves of those whose lives were sacrificed in this rush for wealth, and its history is replete with all that can excite interest and pity. Romance and tragedy are written in every mile and the deep and abiding impressions which this pilgrimage made along this surface of the earth is but a symbol of the deeper and more lasting impression which it wrought upon the life of the nation.[2]

We reached the imaginary village of Bessimer at sundown. This is at the mouth of Parson Spiller creek and just across the river is a large bottom which is in all probability the place where the returning Astorians built their first winter quarters in November, 1812. I spent considerable time in examining the surroundings so as to get a good impression of it for future work.

We reached Casper at 10 pm.

May 14, 1897

Left Casper by rail at 9:30 am and arrived at Cheyenne at 3 am next morning. It was the most exasperatingly slow ride by rail that I ever experienced and caused me to lose the east bound train from this point. The monotony of the day's journey was, however, to some extent relieved by my pleasant conversations with Gov. Richards of Wyo., who gave me much valuable information regarding the State and my work in general.

May 15, 1897

I called on Gov. Richards in the morning and copied some survey plats in the surveyor general's office. At 2 pm left for Omaha. Nothing of interest occurred.

May 16, 1897

Reached S. Omaha at 10:02 am. Called on a Mr. Gibson and then proceeded by the electric line to Omaha. Called on Messrs. Richardson, Baldridge, and Berlin. Also at Hdqrs. Dept., Platte. Left at 4:30 pm via Wabash for St. Louis.

May 17, 1897

Reached home at 7 am.

Journal of a Trip to Jackson Hole and Idaho, August 1897

August 2 - Monday -

Left Union Station via B. and M. at 8:45 pm. Mrs. C. children and self. — Weather intensely hot.

August 3 - En route

Reached Kansas City in morning, Lincoln, Neb. in evening. Met Mr. and Mrs. Wilson en route for Yellowstone National Park. Also saw Mr. Chase, master mechanic B & M Lines, and Mrs. Dent, widow of Col. Dent, brother of Mrs. U. S. Grant. Very hot in forenoon. Heavy rain in pm cooled atmosphere.

August 4

Reached Denver 7:15 — Left at 9:30 am. Reached Lyons 11:40 — Took stage at noon. Reached Elkhorn Lodge, Estes Park, at 6 pm in midst of heavy shower.

August 5

Took a ride around Park with Nettie and children.

August 6

Went down to Cañon where Big Thompson leaves Park. Excellent reservoir site in valley above, but dam site inferior. Not practicable to get dam above 50 to 75 ft. Length probably 600 feet. Capacity of reservoir possibly one billion cubic feet. Abundance of water.

August 7

Took ride up Fall Creek with Nettie and children in forenoon. Fished some — caught 6. Nettie feeling ill, we returned. Fished some in pm. Success indifferent.

August 8

Left Park for Loveland at 7:30 am. Scenery along route fine, particularly view back into Park, and from Bald Mt. forward to the plains, the appearance of which strikingly resembled the ocean. Reached Loveland at 2:30 pm. Took livery at 3 pm for Greeley, passing en route Boys' Lake which my party surveyed early in July. On way a heavy shower came up in rear at foot of mountains, circled to south, and when we arrived at Greeley was in full blast 10 to 20 miles east. Reached station in Greeley at sunset and just at that moment there appeared the most brilliant rainbow in east I have ever seen. Took three Kodak pictures of it, 7, 15 and 30 seconds exposures respectively.

The part of Colorado passed over today is very fine and might compare favorably with agricultural sections of East.

Left Greeley at 8:20 pm arriving at Cheyenne at 10:15 pm.

August 9

Called at State House at 9 am after having done a little shopping for Nettie. Met Gov. Richards and Major Wilhelm. Latter drove me to Fort D. K. Russell at 10:30 am where I met several officers and procured transportation to Sheridan, Wyo. Spent portion of pm in correspondence and in getting records at Surveyor General's office.

August 10

Set out on the morning train on the Cheyenne and Northern for Wheatland where we arrived at noon. Engaged a livery and started at an early hour in the afternoon for old Fort Laramie 30 miles away. Reached there about 2 hours before sunset and rode over the grounds round about with "Jack" Hunton, at whose house I remained over night. It was a sight well calculated to awaken vivid impressions — that of this historic post now abandoned and going to ruins. Some of the noted old buildings are still standing; for example the Bedlam now permanently fixed in story by the pen of Capt. King.

In the house next to that where I was staying, James Bridger used to find lodgings. The old fur trading posts are all gone, but Mr. Hunton showed me where old Fort John once stood. The traces of the old roads are everywhere distinctly visible, and give a strong idea of the travel that once passed by this now deserted point — for deserted it certainly is. As the sun fell behind the Laramie Hills and clothed the prairie landscape in a beautiful half light, there was a stillness everywhere around that was in keeping with this burial place of former activity. It was left for the imagination to fill up the void — to conjure up the far past when the seven returning Astorians passed by the mouth of the Laramie — when the early hunters under Ashley, Sublette and Campbell made their way to the distant mountains, — whence Bonneville and Wyeth and the Missionaries crossed the famous stream whose name Joseph Larémé in those early days gave and consecrated with his life. Then, what hardship, and suffering, of the long period of Californian emigration. Of the eventful period of military occupancy there are mementos, indeed, for the old garrison buildings are still there although now in ruins.[1]

I passed a pleasant evening with Mr. Hunton who greatly enjoyed the opportunity to do a little "reminiscing".

August 11

Set out very early for Wheatland where we arrived before 10 am. Mr. Johnson, Engineer of the Wyoming development company, at once took me to some of their works, particularly a depression reservoir in the vicinity. We returned just in time to get dinner before the train left — at 1 pm.

I found on the train Col. Bacon and family whom I had known in Omaha. The Colonel was en route for Fort Meade to take command there. We arrived at Crawford late in the evening and I took lodgings for the night. Our course on the FE&M RR ran for quite a distance along the upper valley of the White River. I was much interested to find that it is here called the Running Water. As is well known, this stream was long known as *L'eau qui Court*, the early French name. Strange to say the translation of this old name has settled upon that portion of the river which is utterly sluggish and stagnant, while it has disappeared from that portion which is really a "running water" stream.

August 12

Left at 6:30 am on B&M for Sheridan, Wyo. Arrived at Clearwater at 3:20 pm. and went over to Buffalo, Wyo. arriving about 10 pm.

August 13

Next day I went up above old Fort McKinney to fish in Clark Creek with Dr. Lott.[2] Caught 27 trout. That evening Mr. Mead, State Engineer of Wyoming, arrived from Cheyenne.

August 14

Mr. Mead, Mr. Fred Bond and myself set out at 8 am for Bryants Ranch on Rock Creek. There we took a pack outfit and went to a camping place on Big Piney where we slept that night. Had some fine views of the country below.

August 15

Visited Cloud Peak Lake near the eastern base of Cloud Peak. Altitude nearly 10,000 feet. The lake is a beautiful sheet of water about a mile long and between ¼ to ½ mile wide. It is a good reservoir site. The scenery in its vicinity is grand. We returned in the evening and camped on another site some 1000 ft. lower. It was an excellent site for a reservoir and I decided to have it surveyed.

August 16

Mr. Mead and Mr. Bond with two or three others went to get pictures of Cloud Peak from an adjacent peak about 12,000 feet high. I returned to the valley and visited Lake De Smet and took some pictures of it. This lake certainly offers excellent facilities for the storage of water. It has no present outlet and the water is reputed to be bad; but I could detect no bad water and I noticed that cattle drink it with impunity. From Lake De Smet I visited the site of old Fort Phil Kearny in the lovely valley of the Piney — and then went to the locality of the massacre.[3] Got several pictures. Drove through a most interesting irrigated section showing the facility with which rough and rolling country can be irrigated. Also saw a striking example of how creeks and rivers are turned into other valleys than their own for irrigation purposes. The waters of Big Piney are here very largely diverted into the valley of Goose Creek and find their way to the Yellowstone through Tongue River, instead of by their natural outlet, Powder River. Arrived at Mr. Warburton's sawmill at 6 pm. After supper went fishing and caught 13 in a few minutes.

August 17

Was rejoined this evening by Messrs. Mead and Bond. Took dinner at Warburton's and drove to Sheridan in pm arriving at a little after 5 o'clock. There we met the balance of the party who were to make the long journey with us to Jackson Hole. I was busy all this evening attending to my mail and other matters.

August 18

Set out about 10 am on our long journey to Jackson Hole. The party consisted of eight men besides the driver and we had two wagons. There were Mr. Elwood Mead, State Engineer of Wyoming and manager of the party; Harry Hay, State Treasurer of Wyoming; Mr. E. S. Nettleton, an engineer of long experience in Colorado, formerly prominently connected with the U. S. Geological Survey, and for several terms State Engineer of Colorado; Mr. Harrison, a water works engineer of Stillwater, Minn.; Mr. Smiley, Congregational minister of Cheyenne, Wyo.; and Clarence Johnson a young engineer of Cheyenne. We were equipped with four cameras, one large field glass, two hand levels, one [   ], three barometers, one thermometer, and a current meter. Mr. Smiley had also a small spring weighing scale to weigh the fish and game we might capture. There were two shot guns, one rifle and five fishing rods along. There was also one tent which was not used during my stay with the party. We all slept out of doors with no covering but our blankets and tarpaulins. The weather was perfectly clear until our arrival at Jackson Hole.

The party were on the whole congenial, although there were occasional undercurrents of dissatisfaction.

Nooned this day on the mountain side near a fine spring of 39° temperature. Camped at night at Morris Ranch on the road to Dome Lake and ten miles away.

August 19

Arrived at Dome Lake 9:30 am and remained 'til 2 pm. Took several pictures. This place has been turned into a summer resort under the patronage of the B&M RR but it can never be a success as it lacks the essential elements of attractive mountain scenery. The lake itself is surpassed by thousands of mountain lakes. The timber is all burned off its mountains around about, and the means of access are simply abominable. In the afternoon we succeeded in crossing the summit of the Big Horn mountains and encamped on the head waters of Shell creek.

August 20

Last night's camp was a very cold one. I measured the ice on our pail of water and it was fully ¼ inch thick. Our altitude was over 9600 feet.

We had almost no breakfast, and as a consequence most of us had a head-ache when we reached noon camp. In fact, Mr. Harrison was quite ill. We shot 5 birds enroute and luckily fell in with a USGS camp or we should have gone hungry for lunch. In the afternoon made Hyattville on the No. Wood where we remained all night. Our trip from Sheridan across the mountains had an interesting feature in the elevation strata set all along the way by the USGS. The latter part of our route lay among the badlands — a very repulsive tract of country — caught one fish in the evening.

August 21

Encamped at a ranch 4 miles from the Big Horn river where Mr. Mead gauged No. Wood Creek. At 2 pm we forded the Big Horn. Messrs. Mead and Johnson stopped to gauge the stream while the rest of us pressed on to Otto. Region mainly bad lands till we reached the Grey Bull. Arrived Otto a little after dark. Had some difficulty getting horses across river and I had to get out into the creek. Messrs. Mead and Johnson arrived soon after we left.

August 22

Nooned at a solitary ranch house away from the river. Reached the YU ranch at a late hour and slept under a hay stack. This ranch is a very extensive hay ranch.

August 23

Set out at a good hour and arrived at Mulutse at noon. This is one of the most abandoned towns I ever saw. Saloon business was the only prosperous one. Every hotel kept a sporting woman for the convenience of boarders. The first night we were treated to a succession of revolver volleys probably designed to excite the alarm of the tenderfoot. Mr. Smiley and I went fishing in the afternoon and had fair success.

August 24

A portion of the party set out for Franks Ranch leaving the remainder to come on later in the day. In the afternoon Messrs. Harrison, Smiley, Johnson and myself engaged a wagon and driver and went to Franks Fork to fish. About an hour and a half before sunset the driver deliberately pulled out and left all of us but Johnson who had gone down the road hunting and was overtaken by the wagon. When we came out of the brush at sundown and found the wagon gone, we decided to go to Ashworth's (an Englishman) ranch about ¾ of a mile away and across the river. It was long after dark when we got there. We had to remove our shoes and ford the river which was full of boulders. The man in charge of the ranch, a "busted" French dignitary, treated us with scant courtesy and assigned us to the bunk house for lodging and food. Next morning I threatened to inform Mr. Ashworth of his conduct and this brought him to his senses. He could not treat us well enough after that.

Our failure to return to Franks very unnecessarily aroused the alarm of the balance of the party who pretended to fear we were lost. There was however not the slightest possibility of getting lost. They built a bonfire on a hill and fired guns etc. etc.

August 25

Set out next morning up the river to Pickett's, fishing on the way. Arrived there about 10 am and found the venerable proprietor of the ranch, Colonel Pickett, an ex-Confederate and distant relative of Gen. Pickett of Gettysburg fame, a man over 70 years, still active and hearty.

An hour later the balance of the party came up and forthwith set upon us in a very intemperate manner for having failed to show up the night before. Some feeling was displayed. Afterward it was published to have been a concerted joke, each of us to be taken to task for our actions. But it was clearly pretty earnest, and our resentment at the treatment doubtless evolved the joke theory.

That afternoon Messrs. Mead, Smiley, Pickett, and myself went some miles further up the valley to visit the celebrated artist Anderson who has a most unique and expansive ranch here. The place was a very interesting one to visit. Mr. Mead remained here all night and the rest of us returned to Col. Pickett's.

August 26

Party set out early for Mulutse arriving about noon. Mr. Mead followed two hours later. A new outfit was procured here and we stocked up with provisions for regular camping, instead of relying as heretofore on ranch houses. Set out about 4 pm and camped that night on Gooseberry Creek.

August 27

Made our way today across a succession of hills and valleys to [   ] ranch on Owl Creek at the north base of Owl Creek Mountain.

August 28

Crossed the Owl Creek Mountains in the morning, and came into full view of the Wind River Range, a most majestic wall of mountains, although partially obscured by the hazy atmosphere. Camped not far from the foot of the range on a creek whose name I forget.

Our information as to the afternoon route proved entirely erroneous, and although it did not cause us to lose our way, it made us think we had. We encamped at a late hour on Dry Creek within 4 miles of Wind River in a straight line.

August 29 — Sunday

Set out and crossed the point of land between Wind River and Dry Creek, Mr. Mead selecting the road. Nooned in a beautiful grove on the banks of Wind River and remained until 3 pm when we put in a three hour drive and encamped in another place, also on the banks of the river. This stream seemed to me one of the most beautiful I have ever seen, and the valley for many miles appeared to me one of the most desirable in the whole state of Wyoming. It is now an Indian Reservation.

August 30

Route all day up Wind River. Caught a few fish at noon. At evening camp made a good catch, taking one weighing 2 lbs. Fine scenery all day, and fair travelling.

August 31

Horses missing this morning but soon found. Caught several fine trout before starting. Made Union Pass and nooned in small branch of Gros Ventre. Union Pass struck me as a very poor excuse for a *pass* and was selected I imagine mainly because of the broad open space on top where travelling is easy. There was clearly a shorter cut to the right and a lower pass. Caught a glimpse of the Tetons from the summit, a most wonderful and impressive sight. The wind blew a heavy gale while we were crossing.

From the Gros Ventre water shed we passed temporarily to that of the Green river and camped at night where we could overlook the sources of that famous stream. Camp in a bad place and very cold.

September 1

Course all day down branches of Gros Ventre and main stream. Nooned in a small willow bordered creek road bed. Camped at 6 pm on hillside above main stream. I went down to river and made a fine catch of 13 trout one weighing 2½ lbs.

September 2

Messrs. Mead, Hay, and myself set out early for the purpose of taking me to Jackson P.O. where I was to set out for Musket Lake, Idaho. I accordingly bade adieu to the rest of the party who were going to the Yellowstone National Park. Took several pictures enroute and nooned at a small stream near Jackson Hole. Killed 2 grouse at noon camp. Reached Jackson Hole about 2 pm but did not arrive at our destination until 6 pm. Stayed overnight with a Mr. Miller. I had the disappointment to learn that the stage took 3 days to reach Musket Lake and that it would not start until September 4. I had expected to make the distance through in one day. I accordingly hired Mr. Miller to take me across Teton Pass next day to Victor, Idaho whence he thought that I could drive to Musket Lake in one day. Messrs. Hay and Mead spent evening writing letters.

Jackson Hole is certainly one of the most remarkable valleys on earth.₄ In very few places is there so bold and beautiful a mountain scene as is here presented while the lake and beautiful river there lie in the broad flat valley and make a most beautiful picture. The region is still wild and game quite abundant, although the "hole" is filling up with settlers. We saw abundant evidence of the great destruction of elk last winter by the deep snow. I slept indoors for the first time in some days last night. Felt an inclination to catch cold.

September 3

In the midst of a severe rain Mr. Miller and I on horseback, with my baggage on a pack horse set out for Victor, Idaho 25 miles and across Teton Pass. Six miles out we found the dark waters of Snake River, and in three miles reached the foot of Teton Pass. The ascent and descent near the top and for a mile on each side are incomparably the steepest road I have even seen. It appears utterly incredible that a wagon can be hauled up and held back going down. And yet the road is in daily use. It took us some hours to make Victor and of these it rained four. I was well soaked, hat, gloves, shoes, alike full of water while my coat weighed at least 30 lbs. I was exhausted when I reached Victor and was glad to remain there over night.

September 4

Set out early this morning with the regular stage which was driven by a grandson, I believe, of apostle Parley Pratt of the Mormon Church.[5] He got his team over the ground rapidly, and by 2:45 pm we had reached the end of his line at Teton, Idaho, 50 miles. Here I engaged another Mormon to drive me to Musket Lake distant 30 miles. He was an ex-missionary and rather devout. His anxiety to talk on his favorite subject led to a general discussion of Mormon doctrine, and I was frequently amused at the extreme simplicity of the man's character, created no doubt by his dense ignorance of worldly affairs.

We reached Musket Lake at 8 pm. The train did not leave until midnight, and I was so tired that I lay down on the floor in the ticket office and slept soundly until train time. The trip this afternoon took me through a well developed portion of Idaho. I was struck with the great power of the Snake River whose dark green waters seemed a terror to me. I wonder that the Astorians dared to attempt them.

September 5

Took train at midnight. Changed at Pocatello between 3 and 4 am. On train all day arriving at Laramie at 10:30 pm.

September 6

Found considerable mail awaiting me. Attended to this and made arrangements for some work in the vicinity. Left at noon for Cheyenne where I arrived at 2:20 pm. Fixed up my restored trunk and called on various parties. Saw in particular Senator Warren who is managing the reservoir business in Congress, Mr. Coutant who is bringing out a history of Wyoming and a Mr. Cooper who gave me some information about the much discussed question of the ascent of the Grand Teton.

September 7

Visited Fort Russell for my transportation to Cheyenne. Saw Senator Warren again, and also met Mr. Niswander, deputy state auditor with whom I had further discussion in regard to the ascent of the Grand Teton. Lunched at the Cheyenne Club with Messrs. Freborn, Barbour and Henry Hay, Jr.

Left Cheyenne at 2:45 pm and arrived in Denver at 6 pm where I rejoined my family.

September 8

Made a visit to Fort Collins to see Professor Carpenter. Trip successful.

September 9

Went to Golden in morning and returned at 4 pm. Packed trunks and left on 9:50 pm train for St. Louis.

September 10

Enroute all day.

September 11

Arrived in St. Louis 7:19 am.

IV

Notes on

The Reservoir Service

Editor's Notes

In 1906, following the second tour of duty in the Yellowstone, Chittenden was assigned to a survey of reservoir sites in Wyoming and Colorado. This was a territory with which he was eminently familiar as shown in his journal of a trip to this area in 1897.

The great controversies over national conservation were at their height. Chittenden's report to Congress set some of the standards for flood control still in effect. For the historical writer these western travels provided him with further excellent opportunities for pursuing his studies of western development. Interspersed with engineering observations in these "Notes" are such statements as "While on this expedition, I took a great deal of pains to collect historic data on the Oregon Trail and several trading houses, etc., for use in my fur trade work. I made the only survey ever made of Independence Rock and I traveled as far down the Platte as the site of Old Fort Laramie".

Notes on the Reservoir Service contain several salty anecdotes, such as the "fake gold strike", trout-fishing triumphs, and an amusing tale of a buckboard ride with an old Mormon who had certain original ideas about "damnation". Chittenden's unexpectedly humorous gift has certain parallels with the Mark Twain of *Roughing It*.

Notes on the Reservoir Service

THE APPOINTMENT to this particular duty came to me wholly as a surprise. I was officially secretary of the Missouri River Commission, but I cared very little for this duty, because I had seen enough of the Missouri River to have lost all confidence in its future development as a navigable water-way.[1] But the opportunity it gave me of pursuing my historic studies I valued very highly. Now came this other opportunity. The River and Harbor Bill of 1906 directed that a survey of reservoir sites be made in Wyoming and Colorado with certain ends in view. This duty was assigned to Col. Stickney with the indirect view in mind undoubtedly that it would be turned over to me. When the Colonel spoke to me about it I didn't hesitate a minute in saying that that was just what I wanted. And so the matter was settled except that I couldn't get anything like the sum I ought to have had and had to get along with a paltry amount of $5000. This must have been early in the summer of 1906. There were some little embarrassments to begin with. In the first place, my siege of typhoid fever prevented any-thing being done during the summer. Later I learned through Elwood Mead that Senator Warren had expected an immediate report and was very much vexed at the outcome. I wrote to the Senator that I thought that plan the very worst possible to adopt, that the next session was a short session at which nothing could be done and that it would be a great deal better for me to take the year and prepare a thoroughly considered report which he could depend upon with confidence. My illness, of course, was something for which I was not responsible. However, I went at the work with the least possible delay.

As soon as my recovery from typhoid would in any way justify my leaving town I prepared a program for a long trip so planned as to take in the irrigation Congress at Phoenix which was to be held not long before Christmas. I purchased me a good camera and in addition Eastman's cartridge kodak and with this rather formidable array I set forth in due time going first to Denver. I will not go into the details of the trip further than to say that I picked up all the acquaintances that I could, got a great many photographs and gathered a large amount of information. At Santa

Fe I improved an opportunity which I would not otherwise have had to lay in a good stock of historic data.

At Phoenix I attended the Irrigation Congress which had gathered in all the leading irrigation authorities.[2] I took no part, said little, but listened a whole lot; accompanied all the excursions to points of interest, and attracted a good deal of attention by my untiring energy in getting photographs and other data. In fact, not a little fun was poked by Mr. F. H. Newell of the Geological Survey; but he came to the conclusion nevertheless that here was a man to look out for. Mr. J. D. Schuyler, the eminent hydraulic engineer and a very friendly and courteous gentleman, was particularly attracted to me, as was also Mr. W. H. Maxwell who was engaged in the promotion of these ends pure and simple. As we continued our journey to California Mr. Schuyler and Mr. Maxwell, and several other high authorities on irrigation, travelled in the same train. This gave me an opportunity to extend my acquaintance, elaborate the information that I had gathered at the conference and to form an excellent program for my stay in Southern California. Mr. Schuyler took me mainly in charge and with him I visited his very interesting dam at Sweet Water near San Diego and several other interesting structures. One involving a trip up into the mountains, and a hair raising ride down at the tender mercies of a driver of the Yuba Bill type. Why we were not bowled down the mountain a half a dozen times is still a marvel to me. But none of my companions suspected that it was not an experience of huge enjoyment to me. When it is considered that I was scarcely out of a typhoid sick bed, the performance of these two or three weeks still seem to me most extraordinary.

In Los Angeles, Mr. Schuyler entertained me at his home, gave me letters for use on my way north, and we parted in permanent friendship severed only by his death a few years ago. Here the ill experience of my journey began. One very long trip that I made to visit the Tuolomne dam involved a considerable night ride, inconvenient lodgings, and a good deal of chill and cold. The San Francisco climate put the finish on and I started east with a good threat of a case of pneumonia. I was so badly off when I reached Ogden that I went down to Salt Lake City and entered a hospital. Here I stayed for two or three days until the doctor pronounced that I could continue my journey. I picked up some information incidentally and stopped off the train at Cheyenne to consult with Elwood Mead, State Engineer of Wyoming, and at that time the leading authority in our country on the general subject of irrigation. Finally I reached home safely after running a series of risks which I ought to have appreciated and avoided, but Providence still sustained me in spite of my gross violation of the plain rules of common sense.

We were now in early January and I was thankful for the respite of the winter season. The field works were cut down to a minimum and I could devote more time to this special work. I had now collected data enough and talked with people enough and seen enough of the country to enable me to form a very definite idea of what I wanted to do. In fact, while travelling on the train and while in bed I had thought the matter over and over and had worked out quite a definite program. I therefore took hold of the matter at once at St. Louis, organized a working force to do the preliminary work leading up to next season's survey and the whole matter was put into satisfactory motion. I had only a little over ten months in which to complete everything if the report was to be submitted as I had promised. Col. Stickney was very kind to me in authorizing me to utilize the services of James A. Seddon as fully as these could be utilized and not interfere with the regular work. Mr. Seddon was of valuable assistance and I could never have accomplished the work as I did but for his aid.

I had already taken up correspondence with foreign governments, through our state department, asking for general data upon the subject of reservoirs and I was extremely fortunate in securing without very much delay a series of documents from the French government, and from the Russians, of the very highest value. These entered largely into my work.

With the approach of Spring I organized my survey party with the aid of Assistant Engineer F. B. Maltby, and in due time (the exact date I forget) we set out to look over the field. We fixed upon two principal sites and several of less importance for which we thought surveys ought to be made. There were three in northern Wyoming in which I relied upon the services of the State Engineer department of Wyoming. The principal site in Colorado was on the South Platte some thirty miles above Denver and was later developed by the Denver Union Water Co., into what is now the Cheesman Dam. The principal site in Wyoming was at Devil's Gate on the Sweet Water river. With the greater funds of later years the Reclamation Service developed what they called the Pathfinder's site several miles below on the North Platte river. As this collected also the waters of the Sweet Water, it was of course a very much better site. The several parties were organized with a most definite plan as to the amount of work that they must do and the time in which it must be done.

While on this expedition, I took a great deal of pains to collect historic data on the Oregon Trail and several trading houses etc., for use in my fur trade work. I made the only survey ever made of Independence Rock and I travelled as far down the Platte as the site of Old Fort Laramie.[3]

Leaving the parties in the field, I hastened back to St. Louis to resume my regular official duties and continue the writing of my report. I think that Col. Stickney had by this time become a little anxious about what I was doing and I explained everything to him to his apparent satisfaction. He really had to accept it anyway for he had absolutely no substitute to offer. While out in the field, I made tentative arrangements with Elwood Mead to accompany him on a long pilgrimage which he and a party of irrigation engineers proposed to make from Sheridan, Wyoming to Jackson Hole.₄

Later in the summer I took Mrs. Chittenden and the children to Estes Park, Colo., where they remained for a short time and then went down to Denver and took furnished rooms until my return. I then went to Sheridan, Wyo., to meet the Mead party and after the usual delays and preliminaries we started on the long journey. It took us through the Big Horn Mountains down through the Big Horn valley, up the other slope of the valley to Mulutse and other points among the foothills. Mulutse at this time was the last word in the roughness of a cowboy town. In the mountains we met the celebrated mountaineer, Col. W. D. Pickett, and also a very distinguished artist whose name for the moment slips my mind.

My companions evidently regarded me as a sort of odd sheep in the bunch, not a very good mixer, and rather peculiar in my view of things and they sometimes didn't take much pains to conceal their feelings. I had some quiet amusement at one of the camps soon after we started for Wind River. News had come to us some way of the celebrated hold-up in the Yellowstone and it was rumored that the bandits had fled to our section of the country.₅ It was certainly a caution to see the schemes adopted to conceal valuables at night, hunt up safe places to sleep, and take other measures which didn't show any super-excess of physical courage. For my part, I lay right down among the wagons as usual and the whole business did not cause me a feather's weight of concern. Of course, we never saw any trace whatsoever of the bandits. In due time we crossed the intervening range of mountains and came down into the beautiful valley of Wind River, where we remained for a little time. I always felt if I were to take up a ranch anywhere in the central Rocky Mountain region, I should like to take it up in this valley within sight of Crowheart Butte. It is as typical and beautiful a section of the arid regions as I ever saw.

I may mention as we were approaching Wind River, we passed through the tallest growth of sage brush that I ever saw. We stopped to take a photograph and a man standing erect on the seat of the wagon had to hold his hands up to reach the tops of the trees.

After a short delay, near Crowheart Butte, we renewed our course up the river. I do not recall many of the details, but in due time we passed the crest of the Wind River mountains and came over onto the headwaters of the Gros Ventre River and commenced our descent toward Snake River.

We were straggling along in two parties and a little disposed to play tricks on each other. We were quite uncertain as to the road and on the watchout all the time lest we go astray. Our party happened to be ahead and came to where the road divided. We soon found that the two forks of the road came together a little further on, but we put up a solemn notice at the separation directing those behind to take the right hand road. Then we put up a notice at the other end, not quite so solemn, "Aren't you glad you took it?"

In camp that night two things happened, one of which boosted my stock considerably, and the other was the only mean trick played on any one on the expedition. Our party had not distinguished itself as fishermen and had got very pessimistic on the subject. As soon as we stopped in camp and had disposed of our luggage, I took my rod and started out saying that I was going to get some trout for supper. All I heard was some facetious remark that if we didn't want to starve we better not rely on that. I said nothing and started down stream, twilight just coming on. I certainly struck it lucky. The fish were simply jumping over each other to get a chance to bite anything. I stationed myself at the head of a short riffle which smoothed out into a pool below and here went to work, and it was work sure enough. As fast as I cast my line I had a fine trout and before I had gone very far I got hold of the biggest one I had ever hooked and which put me on my mettle to the utmost to land without his breaking off the line, but I finally succeeded, and as I knew the cooks were getting supper, and needed any fish we might get right away, I gathered together the fifteen or twenty smaller trout and this big one and made haste back to camp. The loungers in camp (for everyone was pretty tired) pricked up their eyes as soon as they saw me coming, evidently with something beside a fishing rod in my hand. Entering camp in entire nonchalance I lay my burden down near the cook stove and remarked, "Now I wish some of you other fellows would get these ready for dinner, as I'm pretty nearly fagged out". They were very much astonished indeed and said they would yield the palm to me as fisherman of the trip.

The trick above referred to was played upon Col. Harrison, a member of the party from Minnesota and who had all along had a sort of a tender spot in his heart for me. But he was crazy to do some prospecting and had brought the necessary tools with him. His ardor in testing every gravel bar finally excited the mirth of the party, and Col. Nettleton of Denver, resolved to satisfy his passion for once. The Colonel had two fine models of Alaska nuggets which were simply lead gilded over. Whether he had brought it along for some such purpose or not I do not know, but he didn't show them around much and I think that only two or three of us had yet seen them. While I was fishing the two Colonels were prospecting. Col. Nettleton having offered to coach Col. Harrison a little in the art of panning out gold. The result was that after a few trials in which they actually did get some color as was to be expected in that region, but all of which seemed wonderful to the tyro in that business, the Colonel let the little nugget slip into the pan. It did not escape the eye of the eager Minnesota Colonel. He grabbed it and fairly jumped over himself in his enthusiasm. "Well," said the Denver Colonel, "let's not stop with that." After two or three more efforts in which nothing but ordinary color was obtained, Col. Nettleton slipped in the big nugget, which in due time came under the prospector's eye. This was too much for him. The thing to do was to get right back to camp, tell the good news to the boys and give each an opportunity to stake out his claim. They arrived in camp just about the time the fish were ready to eat. They were received with scoffing and indifference, of course, but Mead and others who recognized the nuggets and saw the successful joke which the Colonel had played, thought it was best to let the matter take its course. All of them, however, were too hungry to stake out claims right off and thought that morning would be time enough. Col. Harrison was a good deal disturbed at this but had to acquiesce and after supper began to pore over his nuggets. He examined them over and over and finally his thumb nail scratched a little beneath the surface. He thought the color didn't look exactly like gold and he explored further. The result was he got up in a tower of rage and denounced the vile trick which had been played upon him. We all looked on in the utmost bewilderment, but Col. Nettleton could not escape. Whether the thing would result in a downright fight or not was quite uncertain for a time, but before next morning the Colonel was somewhat calmed down and we heard nothing further of his prospecting operations.

The next day we made our way over a very tedious road, down the Gros Ventre River and at length came to the famous Jackson Hole where we made for the ranch of one of Mr. Mead's acquaintances. Here we got our first real rest and the next day, which was excessively rainy, we spent in preparation for the rest of the trip. I was to leave the main party here for the purpose of reaching a railroad at its nearest point, Musket Lake, Idaho. The rest of the party were going to take in Yellowstone. We made a proper division of our supplies and Mr. Mead and I straightened up our accounts so that they could be properly settled later. It was evident that, upon parting, my companions had formed a good deal closer attachment to me and respect for my views than at any other point of the trip. The following morning was as rainy as ever but still I decided to set out. I found a man who would accompany me and, protecting myself the best I could, I started on the long ride with a borrowed horse, over the mountains into the valley beyond. It was a most tedious and exhausting trip. The mountain trail was so steep that the horses could scarcely get up it in the slippery mud. When at last we reached the top it was almost like the roof of a house, so quick was the change from one slope to the other. We continued down the western slope and out into the plain where, at some ranch house that I don't remember the name of, we put up for the night. Here I turned my horse over to my escort and he started back the next day. I had some little difficulty in arranging for a conveyance to Musket Lake, Idaho, still seventy miles farther on. But at length I negotiated with a Mormon to take me with his buckboard a little over half the distance where he thought he could find me a conveyance for the rest of the way. As I wanted to make the whole distance in a day, we started very early next morning in spite of my need for further rest.

This Mormon driver was an interesting character in his way. He seemed thoroughly innocent of any education and had become so infatuated with his new religion that he could scarcely think or talk of anything else. The whole forty or fifty miles of our journey together he scrupulously devoted to trying to make a Mormon of me. I made no effort whatever to argue with him but let him ramble on calling him down once in a while on his facts. He came to have a very high respect for my knowledge but grew more and more dubious as to the effect of his proselyting. I did slip in enough talk to beat it into him that I was particularly interested in the subject of reservoirs and dams. The subject of dams gave him a new lead. He said he had his own ideas about damnation. It was not a state of wretchedness, misery and punishment, as many supposed, but a state of damming back our joys and pleasures for a period in order that they might flow out in fuller volume later on. I admitted that was an entirely novel idea to me.

Late in the afternoon we reached our relay point where I settled with my Mormon driver and secured another buckboard to take me to Musket Lake within a specified time. It was getting rather late in the afternoon but the route lay through a very beautiful irrigated district and I was glad that my day's travel was to be rewarded with a sight of something of a really practical nature. I came to observe that whenever we got into these Mormon colonies we encountered a degree of system, orderliness and cleanliness that were in the highest degree to the credit of those simple and religious people.

It must have been nine or ten o'clock when a lone light hove in view which the driver said was the station light at Musket Lake. We were at the station in a little while and after settling with my driver I attended to my tickets and baggage. I then sought out the station keeper and asked him if he couldn't at least give me a board to lie down on, as I had to wait two hours for the train. He rustled up an old mattress, promised to wake me in time for the train and that's all I remember until he called me. Then began the long journey of 1500 miles to St. Louis. I was tired enough to sleep a good deal of the time, but stopped off between trains at Cheyenne to give to the friends of my companions news of our journey. When I reported in the office in St. Louis I think Col. Stickney was a little shocked at my drawn and tanned appearance for he remarked, that now that I had got down to rock bottom I ought to begin to pick up. After a brief explanation of the character of my trip I withdrew to my own office where I quickly resumed with gentlemen Seddon and Maltby the work of getting our report into final shape.

This final work which must be done in a little over two months was indeed very strenuous. I took a great deal of pains in writing the report and repeatedly went over with gentlemen Maltby and Seddon the details of their respective tasks. Mr. Seddon in particular prepared one of the most elaborate monographs upon the floods of the Mississippi and the influence of the several tributaries that has ever been published. Mr. Maltby's work touched exclusively the practical side of our work and he got out splendid maps and drawings and a good report by himself. Mr. Fred Bond, whom I hired to attend the work in northern Wyoming, had his work in on time. Finally, we assembled the whole document, the maps neatly folded and the whole firmly bound together into a document about an inch and a half thick. We prepared it in duplicate. When I took this document in and laid it before Col. Stickney as a result of my work he looked up in evident astonishment. He saw what it had all meant and that I hadn't been wasting any time. I told him that it was important to have it forwarded to the Chief of Engineers as soon as possible in order that it might be ready for submission to Congress in December. The report was submitted November 6th and was forwarded to Washington by Col. Stickney with some comment one week later. I sent a personal letter to Maj. McKenzie in the Chief's office stating that I hoped he would not consign my own report and Mr. Seddon's to the conventional small print of subordinate reports. With this the matter was off my mind as a definite *fait accompli* and I felt the relief of having done a complete thing as nearly to my satisfaction as the circumstances would permit.

In the long course which such documents have to take I had only two or three hints of what its reception might be. The first of these was from Maj. McKenzie who said that Gen. Wilson was very highly pleased and that I could count upon a favorable endorsement. Finally, the work appeared and produced an instant impression throughout the entire West. I did not realize fully how ripe the time was for it. The ground had not before been covered in any sympathetic or comprehensive way but the people grasped at this report as if it were manna from the wilderness. Elwood Mead, who had not been very condescending in his relations with me, wrote that he had never known of a public document to make such a profound impression. Many letters came and I suddenly found myself an authority of high standing on the subject in which a little while ago I was entirely unknown. Mr. George H. Maxwell regularly carried a report with him in his irrigation propaganda work, calling it his "irrigation Bible". Nearly the entire report was reprinted in the Congressional Record in the speeches of Congressmen. The immediate reservoir development which I proposed gave way to the later creation of the Reclamation Service, as was very properly the case, my work being practically done in its arousing of public sentiment.[6] The scientific discussion of the effects of reservoirs upon floods remains to this day, over twenty years, a widely quoted authority. The whole outcome in spite of many disagreeable circumstances, has been one of eminent satisfaction to me.

V

Historical Work

Editor's Notes

The writing of history as history itself is dynamic. Chittenden's account of becoming a historical writer gives us little more than the "bare bones" of the process. That he stimulated much in his readers, and that they, in turn, contributed much help toward his later revisions, is beautifully borne out by the letters from readers printed in the Appendix for Chapter V.

The correspondents were men of no mean historical talent themselves. There are letters from the Reverend L. B. Palladino, the Jesuit historian; the Reverend J. Neilson Barry, a prolific investigator of northwestern history; Mr. W. F. Wagner, scholar from Washington, D.C., successful historical "detective" who located the Last Will and Testament of John Day. Each letter, even today, represents a cache of historical "gold". Light is shed on some of the mysteries surrounding the probable track of the fur-traders, the early missions, the clouded tragedies of opening the West.

Chittenden's engineering career regularly resulted in happy geographical accidents which placed him in the right place at the right time. His assignment to the Yellowstone resulted in his classic work on that region; his work in Missouri Valley reclamation led to the history of early steamboating, then permitted six years of research in the records of the American Fur Company, at St. Louis, which gave us the great *American Fur Trade of the Far West*.

Tracing the process which converted the soldier into historian is a fascinating exercise in sources: the journals evolved into reports, the reports into books, the books generated discussion and correspondence which were helpful in later books and later revisions — in other words, a forceful demonstration of the historical process at work. The imaginative sweep which Chittenden brought to his vision of the West, the thoroughness and the persistence of a determined scholar, combined the three qualities of supreme importance to a pioneering historian. It has been truly said, "He nevertheless found time to publish books on Western history between 1895 and 1905, all of which have stood the test of time to a remarkable degree, subsequent research having filled in detail rather than rendered their conceptions and structure obsolete".[1]

Historical Work

MY ENTRY into the field of historical work was purely accidental. I had become so discouraged over a prospect of ordinary literary work, and still my ambition was so strong to do something in that line, that I felt quite disheartened as to whether to drop all idea of any such work or not. It is only when one runs up against the real thing, and finds how ignorant he is of the intimate experiences of life that he learns how little he is fitted for fiction and similar writings. When he enters the larger field of essay work he becomes appalled at the vast knowledge of all successful essayists. How these geniuses acquire such a range of knowledge has always been an enigma to me. I had some faculty of expression, and if I had some knowledge of facts I could have accomplished much more than I did. It was only when it came to things in which my line of information was special, that I could accomplish real work.

It was in the midst of this discouragement and uncertainty that I conceived the idea of writing the "Yellowstone".[1] It soon came to absorb my interest and it led me into an acquaintance with Dr. Elliott Coues which was perhaps the turning point in this particular line of study. Dr. Coues, famous as he was as a man of science and letters was still very remarkable in his personal characteristics. I was quite astonished at his willingness to help me for he was himself buried deep in his own historic work. His interest ran beyond mere answers to my questions and seemed to extend to myself. It was very clear that he was apprehensive about the wisdom of going into the literary field and more than once he pointed out the difficulties in the way. But as he saw my persistence, he fell more and more into line and was particularly impressed with the thoroughness of my research in the limited field of my inquiries. Later our correspondence developed to a great extent. I have a complete file of his letters and it is astonishing to me that he could ever have taken as much time as he did in writing them all in long hand. But the truth was that as I extended my work I became a pretty valuable source of information to himself and he said once that I was the best correspondent that he ever had.

The completion of the "Yellowstone" book, though somewhat amateurish and freakish, was still quite an accomplishment, and the historical study turned my thought definitely in that direction. So when I was sent to St. Louis in the spring of 1896 it seemed an almost providential confirmation of my desire to write a history of the fur trade; because it placed me at the very seat of the original data upon that subject. With a great deal of consultation with Dr. Coues we agreed that it was the proper thing to undertake but we were very far from agreeing as to what the chronological limits of the work should be. In fact, that point was finally settled only as the work drew near its close.₂

Now began the experience which has been a source of astonishment to me ever since. I didn't care enough about the Missouri River to waste any unnecessary energy thereon, for I felt as certain then as I do now that it would all be labor lost. I, therefore, had no compunction in directing as much of my time as I could to work which I believed would be of a great deal more use to my countrymen. So I started in to unearth data and finally got in touch with the *Chouteaus*, who were the *repositories* of all the *American Fur Company* records. I cannot but wonder that they should have turned over to me as they did the half carload or so of records, dealing with their most intimate concerns of the past; but such was the case, and now I was confronted with the appalling task of going through these records and extracting the fugitive gold from such masses of pure dross. The records were at least two-thirds in French and some in Spanish. The documents were covered with at least three-fourths of the coal iron dust of St. Louis and I had to dress up in workmen's clothes whenever I went to select a package for use. These I examined mainly at my boarding house where I had a little stuffy alcove in which they were sorted over. Extracts were made extensively. When these were brief they were made only on cards, when more extensive they were made in large notebooks for the purpose and in this Mrs. Chittenden rendered me a good deal of assistance in copying. She used to protest vigorously against my giving so much time and strength to the work and very much feared ill results. I remember particularly the day of the St. Louis cyclone. It had been developing all the afternoon and the western sky bore an appearance the most remarkable I had ever seen. Mrs. Chittenden tried again and again to get me to leave my paper and see what seemed to be threatening but I would not until a short time before the storm actually burst. We certainly got enough of it when it did come. I do not remember how long I was getting through this vast mass of papers but it was necessarily a good while and I do not think that any other human being will ever have the courage to do it again.₃ Then there were very many other valuable sources of information. The St. Louis *Republican,* the first St. Louis paper which began its career in 1808, I had looked through line by line down as far as 1840. I will not enumerate the many valuable documents that I came across but every search led to some new find and I began to think at last that I had pretty well mastered the field.

Then followed the writing of the book to which I devoted a great deal of care. I was now entirely alone in the matter for the good Dr. Coues had passed away and I no longer had his friendly criticism. But he had come to have great respect for my research and particularly when I pointed out to him his erroneous conclusions as given, I think, in the Thompson and Henry journals, that the Astorians discovered South Pass. With the completion of the writing, came of course, the question of publication. Here, too, Dr. Coues was indirectly of great help to me because the publishers of his *Lewis and Clark* and *Pike* may not so readily have taken over the publication of my work if it had not been for the confidence of Dr. Coues.

The work was finally published and received the highest praise. I do not think I have ever seen any adverse criticism. It has been often referred to as a great work and has taken its place as a standard.[4] I am fully conscious that in a multitude of details there are inaccuracies which will come to light upon minuter research. If I had taken the time and the work to pin down the last point, unimportant or not, so that I could have said under oath that it was the exact truth, I could never have written the work or I should have so lumbered it over with routine and detail that it should not have been read. On the whole, it is essentially accurate, and it deals with broad outlines in such a way that the average reader follows it with ease and interest. I have never seen any cause to regret the course I have pursued. This work I put down as emphatically a thing done and this view is confirmed as time goes on. The book sells as well today as it did after the first flush of reviews, and it will continue to sell.[5]

As an aftermath of this came my history of Missouri River Navigation, which I felt personally was the most *interestingly written of my books*, but which has never had the popularity of the *Fur Trade*.[6] The monumental work, *The Life and Work of Father de Smet*, I did in collaboration with Mr. A. T. Richardson. It was a laborious work in its routine but involved nothing like the research in preparing for the *Fur Trade*.

VI

Personal Notes

Editor's Notes

Chittenden's "Personal Notes" formed the beginning of an unfinished autobiography dictated to his daughter, Eleanor Chittenden Cress, a few months before his death.

Some of the assumptions which the editor carried at the beginning of this work have been dispelled by the discovery of new material, family interviews, and internal evidence in some of the transcribed manuscripts. Where it had been assumed that the author kept diaries only until the beginning of his Army career, several have turned up which were written during his later professional experiences. Some of this material sheds considerable light upon the importance of Chittenden's records of the formative years in western New York.

This boyhood idyll, an account of his youth in Cattaraugus County, has the zestful bite of a Finger Lakes' apple. In the simple recall of farm and village life in the 1880's, Chittenden weaves a spell with overtones of Mark Twain's boyhood on the Mississippi. His recollections are permeated by some of the quiet philosophy of Thoreau at Walden Pond.

Having been raised in the same beautiful region, the editor can vouch for the absolute authenticity of the narrative. "Sugaring-off" has changed little in the past eighty years, nor have the limestone creeks and lowland marshes with their wealth of flora and fauna altered much. The hills of Cattaraugus County, as much of this early-settled country, are returning to a native state such as must have existed during Chittenden's boyhood. Bear and cougar have been seen once more in the outlying districts, and running a trap-line keeps small boys busy still in the long winter months.

H. M. Chittenden: U. S. Military Academy, Class of 1884

Personal Notes

Seattle, Wash., Mar. 29, 1908

ABOUT FOUR MONTHS AGO my physical condition became so bad that I was confined to my house and have remained there ever since. I have been perfectly clear mentally all the time and as capable as ever of doing mental work, except that it fatigues me more than when in good health. I have carried on my regular official duties, though with a larger share borne by my assistants. In my leisure moments I have looked over my old papers — essays, [maps], diaries, etc. — and have thought it a suitable time to have a good house cleaning, throwing away a great deal of accumulated rubbish, and putting what is worth saving into more orderly shape.[1]

I was surprised to find that I had no record of any sort, in any writing in my own hand, that goes farther back than to 1876, into my 18th year; although I am quite sure that I kept a diary of some sort before that time. The first entry of that character that I can find is November 20, 1878, a little after I had passed my 20th birthday. All my previous doings are, therefore, mere matters of memory, and my account of them will probably be pretty inaccurate; but I shall ask my mother to check up its narration.

When my parents were married they settled on a farm of about seventy acres and commenced life in a log house; but soon after moved into a small one story frame house, and in this, I was born.[2] I still carry a very faint picture of it in my mind. It was about 30 feet long and 18 or 20 wide, with the door (outside) about in the center. Whether there was an addition, or "L", I cannot remember; but it was a perfectly simple frame structure, without ornamentation of any sort. I don't think it had clapboards, and I doubt if it had shingles at first.

All I can definitely remember about the interior is that on the left as we went into the house was the parlor, or room which was occupied least of any; and it seems to me that back of this, and opening out of it, was a bedroom.

The location of this farm was in the town of Yorkshire, County of Cattaraugus, State of New York.₃ It was four and one half miles from the nearest Post Office, and three fourths of a mile to the school house of its district to which it belonged. That country was then very new; and a great deal remained to be done in clearing it up and reducing it to a state of cultivation. Of its seventy acres on the farm, not more than a third was cleared and fit for cultivation when my parents moved upon it. I always thought the farm attractive, topographically. It lay in the valley of a very small stream, which had its several sources not more than a mile from our house. The head of the valley was closed off by a hill which connected with those on each side, completely enclosing the valley on three sides. As these hills were all forest-clad, our horizon was very limited — say a half to three fourths of a mile away. To the eastward the valley opened out into that of a larger stream flowing north and we could see to the fourth side of this valley, with a horizon 6 to 10 miles away. To the eastward was, therefore, our only extensive vista. We could see the sun rise as early as anywhere, but we never had a late sunset.

It is interesting to note how deeply these early impressions become fixed in one's mind, particularly when the whole of one's early life is spent in such a narrow compass. North, east, south and west will always be referred by me to that locality. If I am ever confused in directions momentarily, and have occasion to orient myself into proper adjustments, I go back to the home of my childhood and the whole matter is straightened out at once — the sunrise here, the sunset there, and north and south in their proper places.₄

I have often wondered, since I left the farm, how we lived there so long and made so few migrations into the surrounding country. There were many places within three or four miles that remained to me almost *"terra incognita"*. We very rarely got further away from home than Yorkshire Center or (Machias) — four and a half miles east — in the "Forks of the Creek" where the two tributaries of the Cattaraugus came together — five miles away — or Sardinia, seven miles — or to Ashford to the west, four miles. Very remote places were Springville, where there was an "Academy"; Arcade, where there was another, and also, as I discovered many years later, where my future wife lived; and Franklinville, where there was another Academy, from which I was yet to graduate; and Ellicottville, which I scarcely ever saw. These four places were N.W., N.E., S.E. and S.W. from home and ten to eleven miles away. Possibly once a year we ventured that far from home, and a great event it always was. It was like covering the continent. Still farther away was Olean, Little Valley (the county seat) and Salamanca, 20 to 25 miles distant, altogether too far for my juvenile peregrinations. Still farther (35 miles) was Buffalo, a very dream, where streets were paved and buildings were so thick as to stand close together, and there were railroads and ships and such other wonders to my youthful imagination.₅

It is hard to account for this localized habit which kept me always in such a narrow circle, except it be that farmers in that new country rarely had money to travel with and the needs of their business rarely took them away from home. The hard character of their life kept them and their children always at work when the children were not in school, and thus the whole of life revolved in a very small circle.

Yet no one would even suspect, unless he had been similarly situated, how much there was in this narrow environment that made it an ideal world for children. It was not so much the deficiencies of the locality as the lack of time (on account of work) that made it somewhat irksome to our youthful spirits. We had abundant forests, and beautiful forests, too — the true sugar maple, the birch, brice, cherry, ash, basswood and other deciduous trees. The oak did not grow there. Hemlock was our only evergreen, but a fine tree it was.₆ All around us, some twenty miles away, pine used to flourish, but for some reason not in our township. There was, however, a strange and very interesting freak in the form of a "pine swamp" which occurred here and there in this pine-less country. One of these swamps lay within a half mile of our house. It covered perhaps forty acres and was a true swamp, evidently formed by the filling up of our old pond with vegetable growth. Everywhere there were stagnant pools and the ground was a soft springy mass of vegetable mold which would sink from two to six inches under one's step. The swamp was full of shrubbery among which was an excellent variety of huckleberry. But the most interesting vegetable product of the swamp was the wintergreen. Many a time every spring did we go to the swamp and gather the tender new green plants to eat. The young man could pay his best girl no finer compliment than to give her a bunch of these tender leaves. The swamp also yielded a flowering shrub, of a somewhat sweetish odor; the name of the plant I have now forgotten, or really never knew. Add to these "products" the pitch from the pine trees which we made into gum, and it is readily seen that the Pine Swamp was a resort of no small importance to our little neighborhood.

The swamp lay on the edge of a heavy forest which lay to the south of our farm and extended far beyond it in every direction. On the extreme southern border of the farm, in the heavy woods, across a little rivulet which flowed southward half a mile or so and was there joined by a similar stream from northwest after which the rivulet streams flowed easterly and finally emptied their waters into one of the main branches of Cattaraugus Creek, which, changing its course to a westerly direction, flowed into Lake Erie. We used to call this local stream Big Creek, because, I suppose, it was the largest creek in the vicinity. It was a beautiful, clear stream, once filled with trout and was the scene of many a youthful fishing excursion. About a mile east of our farm it came out into a clearing where it was joined by a smaller, though considerable, stream coming from the northwest. Just below the junction, in a narrow part of the valley, an enterprising citizen by the name of James Hall, had built a dam and a saw mill. This establishment was in many ways of great importance to our little neighborhood. It was very useful in sawing out the lumber required for building, and later for fences when boards began to take the place of rails. It was used a great deal (or rather the capacious mill race was) to wash sheep in before shearing. It was used by the itinerant preachers who visited the neighborhood and preached in the little schoolhouse near by, for the baptism of such converts as their labors procured. But to us boys it was of never ending interest in many ways. Its simple, crude machinery, particularly its great overshot wheel hidden in the dark central recess of the mill, was a perennial source of wonder, and we considered it rare good fortune when the millman would permit us to get to some point of vantage and see in the dim light the great arms of the wheel moving so majestically and see the white foaming water flow away at the base. The saws, too — both the upright for sawing boards, and the circular for sawing shingles, were a great wonder. Indeed, it was a matter of general interest to the whole community when the business of the mill grew so that the old up and down saw was replaced by the large circular saw.

In addition to the interest of the mill itself, the race and pond were great resorts for swimming in summer and skating (for such as could own skates) in winter. In fact it was the only body of water in the neighborhood available for these purposes. Occasionally fine trout were caught under the dam where its overflow ran away, but these places were fished too much to afford good trouting.

While speaking of this establishment I will relate a little incident that will always remain in my memory. Mr. Hall was a rather stern, arbitrary, blunt-spoken man and we boys were a little afraid of him. He rather encouraged this reputation for it saved him from many annoyances which our innocent mischief might otherwise have caused him. One day my brother and I and our uncle, Frank Wheeler (only a few years older than I, and really one of our companions) were on the dam where the sluice ways were provided to let the overflow water pass off when the creeks were high. In the dry season — as at the time of this incident — the flash boards were shut down tight to save all the water, for scarcely enough flowed in by night to keep the mill going during the day. It was, therefore, very important not to waste any. But the sight of the smooth waterfall when the flash boards were up, was a very beautiful one and the temptation to raise the boards and let the water flow was very great. On this particular occasion, Uncle Frank lay down on the bridge over the gates, and reaching down raised up one or two of the flash boards and let the precious water flow away in beautiful cascades and torrents — to our delight, but to the dismay of Mr. Hall. Presently we saw the irate mill-owner coming out from the mill in our direction, but he was unusually pleasant and quite threw us off our guard. He talked with us about the water and finally said he couldn't afford to let so much of it run to waste and told Uncle Frank that he had better shut down the gate. Uncle Frank lay down on his face and reached down to replace the boards, when Mr. Hall, quick as a flash, whipped out a brand new shingle, jumped on to the helpless marauder and gave him a fearful drubbing, paying not the slightest attention to his yells which were loud enough to raise the whole neighborhood. After this punishment he cautioned him not to meddle with the dam any more. My brother and I stood by in speechless terror, expecting that our turn would come next. Why we didn't run I don't know unless we were relying upon our actual innocence in the matter. At any rate Mr. Hall paid no attention to us.

Perhaps the feature of the landscape, or rather the topography, of our farm was the wooded hills that comprised so large a portion of its area. It is indeed, a matter of the deepest pity that the people of the world cannot enjoy, more than they do, the pleasures of the native woods. The flowers and plants of spring, the delicious "ground nuts", the soft birch buds, the wet birch bark; and later the deep rich foliage of summer, the wild berries of all kinds in the cut-over areas, and in autumn the carpet of fresh-fallen leaves, the nuts, the colors of low shrubs, the fat squirrels and the indefinable beauty of the world getting ready for winter; and finally the forest in winter, the soft singing in the trees by the winds which were raging blizzards outside, the still sifting of the snow, the comparative warmth when it was bitter cold in the open, the tracks of squirrels, and coons and foxes, the clear sparkling streams which we loved to drink from even in winter, all remain fresh and ineffaceable in memory.

One feature of our life that related to the woods and which was the most interesting feature of our country life to me was the making of maple sugar in the spring. The long, cold snowy winters where we lived were very severe and trying, and we used to listen and look eagerly for every harbinger of spring. It almost makes me shiver still to see the deep frosted panes of glass, the hills of snow outside, the lines of branches or sticks along the fields to mark new roads after the drifts had driven travel out of the regular highways, and the many other features of those dreaded winters. The daily task of going to the barns at such times to do the "chores", the cutting of the ice in the creeks to let the cattle drink, the bringing in of the wood, etc., were often tasks that shivered us children up to a pink. And then the going to bed at night in a cold frozen chamber with frost gems for electric lights and the soft flow of snow driven through the roof by the blast to add to our covering as the night wore on, and then the ordeal of dressing in the morning in such an atmosphere, all these things made us welcome spring and notice with joy every indication that came along.

The beginning of the flowing of the sap was such a happy augury. The first sap was always best, but it often came so early that it was hard to get through the woods with the snow still deep. The trees themselves seemed to rejoice in the coming of the spring. There would always come a certain stage in the approach of warm weather when the "frost" would "come out" of the trees, and at such time the forest would literally be alive with sharp sounds as frequent as the voices of frogs in a pond on a warm spring evening.

How well we came to know the maple trees. I think there were upward of 300 in our "sugar bush", yet I knew every one by sight, knew its sap-yielding qualities, knew when to expect a full bucket and when one only half full and felt as well acquainted with them as with the cattle in the barn.[7] And what a place did the maple sugar itself fill in our lives! The characteristic flavor of the genuine, pure syrup or sugar I still think surpasses all other things of its kind in nature. Its preparation was carried out in a variety of forms. The syrup was a great reliance. For eating, when "sugaring off", we were very fond of the "wax" formed by pouring the hot syrup, just as it was approaching the consistency of sugar, upon snow. Nothing could excel the delight of this confection; although my personal choice favored the sugar itself "stirred down" until it was almost white. The quantities which we used to eat both during the sugar season and afterward no doubt subjected our stomachs to a heavy strain. The main bulk of the [   ] product was stored in large tubs, and, of course, the earlier portion would be in the bottom of the tub. As the earlier sugar was always clearest and best, the later product becoming colored as the trees began to bud, we used to have to wait until the poorer quality at the top of the tub was used up before we got to the really fine article. This we came to call the "third sand", from a parallel with boring for oil in the oil regions just south of us. The rich liquid was generally formed in the "third sand", as it was called, and we appropriated the term to our own uses. This "third sand" sugar was very much in demand. Our dinners at school or in the woods when we were too far away at work to return for dinner, were often made up entirely of large slices of Mother's fine bread with fresh butter from our dairy all covered over with a thick light yellow layer of the "third sand". No more toothsome morsel ever delighted tongue or palate.

Two incidents connected with this important product of our farm remain in the memory of our family and are worth recording. One related to a fine and much-liked shepherd dog that we owned. He was fond of sugar and one day I took as large a chunk of newly-made wax as he could get in his mouth and then with my hands chucked his jaws close together over it, his teeth being fused into the thick mass. For a time (until the wax softened up) it was impossible for the dog to open his mouth at all for his teeth stuck tight. The poor frightened animal forgot the delight of the sugar in terror at this situation in which he found himself and ran about wildly, whimpering and scratching and performing such antics that we boys nearly laughed ourselves sick. We did not at all appreciate the cruelty of our action at the time. The other incident discloses a not very creditable trait on my own part — that of pilfering good things to eat from our pantry or cellar or wherever else they were kept — and it taxed my mother's ingenuity to find hiding places that would circumvent my ingenuity in searching them out. My particular weakness was a combination of cookies and maple syrup. On the particular occasion in question I had gone into the cellar where the stock of syrup was kept in recesses provided in the cellar wall. Here, too, was a large jar in which the cookies were kept. The convenience of the combination was all that could be desired. For several days I had been there, taking the fruit jars in which the syrup was hermetically sealed, unscrewing the top and drinking out a quantity. I was careful not to reduce the depth in any jar more than an inch or two, lest it be too easily discovered. On the day of the incident I accidentally let a jar slip and fall. Luckily it did not break, and quick as a flash I put it back in its place and hastened to some other place in the cellar. My mother heard the noise and hastened to the cellar door. As she opened it, I called out, "Scat" in vigorous tones and pretended to be engaged in driving a cat out of the cellar. I do not yet understand how this ruse worked so well nor why my mother did not inquire how I happened to be on hand in the cellar looking after trespassing cats.

I was rather alarmed in spite of my lucky escape and seized the first opportunity to cover up my tracks more completely. Taking some water I filled up each of the jars from which I had taken syrup and left everything apparently in its original condition. The incident was forgotten except by myself. Some weeks later my mother brought up a jar of syrup for the table. It was one of those which had been tampered with. The consistency of the syrup had been completely changed by the water. It had become "ropy" or stringy and so unlike the ordinary syrup that no one would eat it. Other jars were tried and quite a number were found ruined, though, strange to say, jars standing side by side with these were found in perfect condition. Circumstances caused a great deal of speculation, both on account of its mystery and the loss, which was considerable. I sagely gave my explanation though I have now forgotten what it was. After a time this feature of the episode ceased to be a live topic.

Something like two years afterward when my brother and I were away in Franklinville at school, I told him the facts under a pledge of secrecy; but he immediately turned state's evidence and told mother as soon as we got home. The offense had so far [   ] that disciplinary measures were not resorted to, but "ropy-molasses" is to this day sufficient to "point a moral and adorn a tale" whenever [   ] arises in our family circle.

As our fuel was wood exclusively, and as it was all out on the farm, we children were trained in the practical use of the axe and saw. I always liked the axe and always retained a good degree of skill in using it. In far later years in my professional work, I had often taken the axe out of a workman's hand to show him how to handle it.

Birch and maple were almost our exclusive reliance for wood except that hemlock and sometimes basswood were used for kindling. No other wood did so well as birch and maple. They chopped easily and split well and made the best of fires. I always thought that father made a mistake in not cutting his wood supply a year in advance so that it might season. The use of green wood was a great nuisance. Another mistake that was always being made was to [   ] the length of the sticks so much that they frequently exceeded the length of the stove. It was then necessary to leave the stick protruding somewhat which spoiled the draft and caused the stove to smoke. Sometimes the wood was sawed, sometimes chopped. Preparing it was always genuine work and therefore, unpopular with us boys. Bringing in the wood every evening until the woodbox was piled high was a part of our regular routine.

Sawing logs for a mill was another important part of our work. These were generally from the hemlock trees, though to some extent from the cherry, ash, and basswood; rarely from the birch or maple in those days, though in recent years these trees have nearly all been cut off. The hemlock trees were usually felled in early summer so as to save the bark which was readily peeled at that season. My brother and I, while still quite young, used to fell and peel large trees, sometimes three and four feet in diameter. It seems to me to have been pretty large work for small boys. I remember that on one occasion we had to cut down a tree against which a large birch had fallen, the lower part of the hemlock being so completely buried in the birch top that it would have been necessary to clear the ladder all the way before we could get at the hemlock at all. As this would have been quite a job, we quietly took some board from a fence and made a little platform on the limbs of the birch top some fifteen or twenty feet above the ground. Here we stood and handled the saw (we always felled these trees by sawing) and succeeded in cutting the tree down. There was some danger at the end lest we should not be able to get off our platform and out of the way before the great tree crashed down on the birch top. We did this successfully, however, and it was well we did, for the hemlock crushed the birch top flat to the ground and our platform with it and there stood its stump towering into the air without rhyme or reason for its being there. Father happened in the woods soon after and I shall never forget his attitude as he came to a standstill in presence of that stump. Clyde and I were busy peeling the bark from the big trunk and kept right on with our work as unconsciously as if we did not know what was puzzling father so. He stood and looked at that stump for fully a minute and then asked gruffly how we cut the tree down at that height. We explained the situation, but instead of being praised for our ingenuity we were severely reprimanded for wasting so much good lumber and bark. In fact we had to cut a log off the stub and peel it.

I remember another incident connected with the peeling of these huge trees. It is a good deal of a sight to see a large tree fall in a deep forest. The loud cracks, about like a small cannon report as the tree begins to move and the big fibres snap under the strain; the graceful (at first) and rapid (later) merging of these reports into a continuous roar; the apparent efforts of the neighboring trees to dispute the right to fall through them, and the fierce and lordly might with which the slain monarch forced his way through them; the relentless crushing of whatever stood in its way, and then the mighty rebound from the earth as it struck with a thunderous roar and a shock that could be felt for great distances, while the air was filled with dust and debris as the mighty tree sank to rest — all made a scene of terrible majesty which we boys always tried to see if we could. The roar of a tree-fall could be heard for miles.

On the occasion referred to we had worked all one day at a very fine tree — a tall stately hemlock, between four and five feet through, and one of the best in our woods. It was nearly noon next day before we had reached the point where the saw cut began to spread showing that the tree was beginning to move. We had with us a fine shepherd dog that we thought a great deal of — too much, as it seems to me now, to permit of the mean trick we then played on him. Seeing the tree would soon fall, I went back to a safe distance, put my arms securely around the dog, as if caressing him, but holding him fast. Presently there came a sharp but loud crash as the first splinter gave way. The dog started in fright and drew every muscle to its utmost tension. Another crash and the dog tried to get away. Then a rustle and movement among the limbs above as if the skies were about to fall. Crash after crash, the breaking and crushing of limbs and the pulling of those broken off, soon threw the dog into the greatest terror. But I held him fast until the great tree was well on its way, the air filled with a deafening roar and the whole aspect of nature in that immediate vicinity there of an [   ] cataclysm of some sort or other. I was unable to hold him any longer and as he broke away he took up such wild and unrestrained race to get out of the forest before the tree fell, that we stood and watched him nearly bursting with laughter and quite unmindful of the vast and awe-inspiring spectacle that was taking place in the other direction.

We were sorry for this bit of wickedness afterward, for we found it impossible to keep the dog with us after this when we were at work in the woods.

I recall in our woods one very remarkable tree — an elm — by far the largest I have ever seen. It was at least seven feet across the stump, was quite free of limbs for upward of seventy-five feet and its top spread out into a vast umbrella. For some reason, it was cut down, though I doubt if it paid for it was so big that it was almost impossible with our crude appliances to get it to mill. These were the days when forests were still an encumbrance to the soil, when the great desideratum was to get rid of them and get the soil under cultivation, where "logging bees" were a regular thing, and any notion that forests protected the soil or saved the water was unthought of.

The first event that remains in my memory was my father's going away to the war.[8] I was about three years old. I remember that mother told me I must not cry until father was gone, and accordingly I braced back against the wall and kept my composure until father left the house.[9] I remember my uncle's coming home on furlough — principally because he played the fiddle and that was a very great treat to me. I remember the day that Uncle George came to our house at the close of the war, calling a considerable distance from the house that Lincoln was killed.[10]

Little events mixed in about this time still rest in my memory. I recall when mother brought home the first Kerosene lamp, my first reader, etc. My grandfather Wheeler lived a mile below us on a side road a quarter of a mile from the main road. The village where we bought supplies and where the post office was, was three and a half miles further on. The lamp was bought in the winter, I being left at grandmother's while mother went to town. It was after dusk when she returned and we were all bundled in the sleigh, sitting down on straw in the bottom, for the cold ride of a mile (how long it was then) to our house. I remember with what care the glass lamp was held — a lamp that did service for many years thereafter. Up to that time we had no other light than that of candles. The running of candles in molds, or making them by dipping was then a very important part of our routine life. Matches were not then so cheap as to make it not worth while to economize in their use, and we regularly cut little hemlock splinters to light from the stove fire and thus light the candles or lamps.

How very primitive our conveniences of that time now seem to us!

It was many years after this time, certainly not fewer than twelve, that Clyde and I brought home as a present to mother the first washstand set for her bedroom. We got it into our guest room through the window and waited for mother to find it, and found our reward in the surprise and tender delight that brought tears to her eyes. Before this time we had only tin dishes to wash in.

Speaking of guest rooms recalls a peculiarity of farm life which seems somewhat strange now though it was based on good and sufficient reasons. The parlor and the parlor bedroom were almost forbidden rooms in the farm houses of that time. The crude ornamentation and luxuries of life were lavished upon these two rooms. Generally the parlor was the only room to have a carpet. Except when "company" came these rooms were kept tightly closed, the curtains drawn tight, and if the house was rich enough to have "blinds" these also were closed. It was a room for "company". The family never lived in it and the children were forbidden to go into it. This seems very strange, but when it is considered how dirty the life on a farm is, how much is dragged into the house, how the dirt from the barns and other places found its way in, it was clearly impossible to have a really clean room except in that way.

I have a very slight recollection of learning my letters which was mainly accomplished by aid of the wall paper, consisting wholly of newspapers pasted on the walls. At that time the walls were not plastered at all. I did not go to school early, not until long after I knew how to read. I think I was about seven — old enough so that Clyde, who was two years younger could go with me. The school house of our "district" was centrally located (to satisfy the jealousies of the citizens) and this "central" location was on a side road on a steep hillside and wholly isolated from any other buildings. A more bleak and lonely spot it would be impossible to find. The district was small and poor and the school house — a little "red" one — was as primitive as the district. As I recall it, it was built upon about this plan. *(Diagram follows in manuscript — not reproduced here. Editor's note.)*

I still have grave doubts as to the real value of such a school as this, and I understand that this one has been abandoned. There were only ten to fifteen pupils on the average. The very lowest wages for teachers was all that could be afforded and so we got the very lowest grade of teachers. There was nothing to give life to the teaching and necessarily disorder and lack of discipline and even absolute immorality were the result. For myself, it was a regular thing to run away and go fishing, take my whipping next day, and do the same again. Numbers of our teachers did not know as much as their best pupils. I remember particularly a tall red-haired girl who had somehow managed to get a "third grade certificate" to teach, and

whom it was my particular delight to mix up in arithmetic. I am sorry now
for it was a terrible ordeal to her. I forget whether it was she or some other
teacher (they were all women) who undertook one day to carry her authority
outside the school room and school hours. Our teachers always "boarded
around", that is, lived with one family and then another according to the
number of children sent. At this time the teacher was boarding at our house
and we were going home together after school and other children going our
way were with us. Clyde and another boy had picked up some butternuts
under one of our neighbor's trees and were cracking them (or trying to)
by throwing them violently against large stones that lay along the road.
Several times the nuts had glanced or rebounded and came near hitting the
teacher or the other pupils. In fact, it was getting to be something of a
nuisance when the teacher told the boys to stop. But the boys feeling that
the teacher no longer had authority paid no attention whereupon she took
the very unwise course of trying to catch and discipline them. She had her
knitting work in her hands, and I think was industriously at work on her
way home. The roads were muddy. The outcome of a race between long
dresses and knitting work on the one hand and two nimble lads on the other
can be imagined. The knitting work fell in the mud while the ball of yarn
stayed in the pocket and unwound until a hundred feet or so dragged on
the ground. Muddy shoes, bedraggled clothes, ruined knitting work and the
culprits still out of reach cracking their butternuts on the rocks! The teacher
can hardly be blamed for entering a complaint with the parents as soon as
she reached the house, nor the parents for siding with her and calling the
boys to account.

I cannot say that this school ever resulted in any real benefit. The moral
tone of the neighborhood was reflected in the children and as I look back
I can see what risks are run in schools of that sort. Owing to the inferior
grade of teachers, it became necessary at an early date to go elsewhere, if
I were to learn anything, and arrangements were finally made to attend the
school in the adjoining district. This schoolhouse was a mile and a half east
of our house at an important road junction known as McKinstry Hollow.
This was a comparatively important school, as district schools went in that
county. There were forty or fifty pupils and in the winter, when older pupils
attended who had to work in the summer, a man teacher was employed.
I remember with what considerable dread I went there, for it seemed a grand
place compared with our humble school, and, of course, we were looked
upon a little in the nature of provincials. But I found no trouble in swinging
my end of the mental work with the rest of them and in a short time my
school standing was assured. But this very fact aroused more or less jealousy
on the part of the regular attendants at the school and it took some time
for this feeling to allay itself. I remember particularly when I went to the
head of the large spelling class on the word *ecstasy*, skipping grown up men

and women who were seven or more years older than I, and I remember how hurt I was when one of the best of them sneered at me after school (when I expected a word of praise) saying: "You think you're awfully smart, don't you?" I was not fitted to cope with this sort of spirit. Jealousy of inferiors with me generally took the form of mental depression, or a feeling of discouragement because I could not come up to the work, and I could not understand how it could take the form of ill will.

At this school I never got into trouble from misbehavior but once. Our teacher was a tall strong man by the name of Sherman — a man of considerable intellectual power and some education, but, as I later came to know him, devoid of real moral worth. At this time, however, he commanded my respect, fear and even reverence, and as I generally had my lessons, he liked me. He used to call me "Hiram, King of Tyre". On the day in question, I had asked permission to sit with my cousin, Arthur Brown, a little while. This was one of the regular privileges granted to pupils on proper occasions. Arthur and I, pretending to be bent over our maps and studying them, had marked out a "fox and geese" diagram and were actually playing that game on our knees under the desk. We became very much absorbed and quite oblivious to what was going on around us. The teacher evidently became suspicious that it was not all study with us. Quietly passing up an aisle some distance from us, he crossed over in the rear of us to the aisle that passed our desk, and then moving noiselessly down upon us verified his suspicions as to what we were doing. The first thing I knew of his presence was the feeling of a powerful grip on my collar and an irresistible force lifting me out of my seat. Instantly I saw that another grip held my cousin by the collar in the same way. In a moment we were out in the aisle, each held by a powerful hand, and being marched down to the front. Here we were forced about, not any too gently, and left standing in the presence of the school, after a few severe comments upon our dishonorable action.

It is now quite impossible for me to understand how deeply this event affected me. My record for behavior had been perfect, and I was considered an exemplary pupil. To be thus paraded without warning, in the presence of the school in this humiliating fashion, as a culprit, completely overwhelmed me. I thought my reputation gone forever. I thought of what my parents would think. I expected some stern and severe punishment — possibly dismissal from the school. Everything grew mountain high and I could not retain my tears. It was wholly impossible for me to see the humor of the situation; to realise that playing "fox and geese" in school was no heinous crime, or to see what a lot of fun the teacher was having, and that he really did not intend to carry the matter further. I had fallen from my pedestal, and that was all I could think of. At the *other* school, it would all have passed as a matter of course.

I may note here some of the little customs of our schools in those days. The going after drinking water was one of the duties or privileges (depending upon the point of view) of the pupils. Twice a day a pail of fresh water had to be brought, and at our little school we had to go nearly half a mile to get it. When the weather was fine and school work irksome (as it always was at such time) applications for this privilege were numerous and the teacher had to keep a regular roster so that no one would be dealt by unfairly. At other times, when too cold or hot or stormy she had to require or enforce the task as a duty.

I have retained all my life a physical deformity that resulted from this duty. We always went barefoot to school in the summer times. On one occasion, while after the water, I stubbed the next-to-the-big toe of my right foot against a stone. It hurt me severely and continued to pain me for a good many days. No examination of it was made, and it was not until after it had gotten well that I found (too late) that the last joint of the toe had become dislocated and the short end bent down nearly at right angles. The deformity has never caused me the slightest inconvenience.

The privilege of "going to the stove", "going to get a drink", "going out", "going to sit with some other pupil", were all a part of our recognized life. The spirit of study could not thrive in such an atmosphere. The inter-mixture of girls and boys in the same seats was not a good thing. In fact the primitive schools of our fathers would not be of much use in the strenu-ous intellectual work of the schools of the present day. A little incident, though quite important to me at the time, occurred when I was quite young — I cannot now remember the exact age. There were two "bad" boys in our neighborhood whom our people were much opposed to our playing with. But as bad boys like bad grown-up folks, are generally most interesting, we (my brother and I) liked to play with them. On this particular occasion, we had been sent to pick berries, and had been cautioned to avoid these two boys if they happened to be out on the same errand. They *were* out and we promptly affiliated with them and the elder of the two (about my age) and myself undertook to have some fun by bending down a maple sapling, getting thereon and teetering. But presently we lost our balance, fell off, and my playmate came down on my left arm in some way so as to break it between the wrist and elbow. When I got up off the ground my arm had the shape of the spout of an old fashioned coffee tea kettle. The pain was, of course, intense and it was a pretty tedious journey home of half a mile or more. Then there was no doctor within about 5 miles and whether the one sent for would be found at home was a question. The accident happened about 10 A.M. and it was 3 or 4 P.M. before the physician arrived. There were no anaesthetics given on such occasions at that time and the doctor took hold of my arm with both hands and simply pulled the kinks out of it regardless of my yells. The bone did not really break until this straightening when it was plainly heard to snap as it was set. It took several weeks for my arm to recover but the recovery was a thorough one and from that day to this I have never been able to tell one arm from the other in the matter of physical perfection. Of course, the moral lesson was quite obvious, though my parents, out of consideration for my misfortune did not press it very strenuously.

A little incident which happened when I was still quite young has remained in my memory because of its unusual character. While out in our pasture one clear mid-summer afternoon between 4 and 5 P.M., the sun still well above the horizon, I saw a "shooting star" — a meteor — pass across the southwest quarter of the sky, leaving a brilliant streak behind it. The meteor appeared almost as large as the sun and almost as bright and sank behind the woods that shut off the view in that direction. I told my parents what I had seen and they, of course, were very skeptical. I happened to be feeling not well the next day and my mother was a little disturbed lest what I had seen or imagined was a portent of disaster.

I do not recall much of my very early reading, but I distinctly remember my deep absorption in the news of the war of 1870 in Europe.[11] Father took the New York Tribune and I used to absorb every word of it. It was about this time that the Tribune published Victor Hugo's *Ninety-three*. I was completely carried away with it and could scarcely wait for the paper, go into the parlor bedroom, lock the door, and read that wonderfully thrilling story of which the names Gauvin and (Cinnourderin) remained ineffaceable in my memory. Many years afterward I procured this work in French, but found it the most difficult reading I had met with in that language — on account of its large number of technical and unusual words and expressions.

We had very few books and those we did have were often of a religious trend. I remember particularly *Mother's True Stories* which I think father sent back from the war; and *Among the Pines*, a story of slavery which impressed me a great deal. Another book did service in our house for many years — until it wore out, in fact — was what we always called the "Indian Book". I don't know what its correct title was, nor who the author was. But its exciting stories and pictures were a never ending fund of interest to us children.

The first real interest I took in poetry was in that of Burns. My mother used to sing *Highland Mary*, and that and some other stray pieces attracted me and after awhile I succeeded in getting hold of a copy. I read and reread and came to know many of the poems by heart. The fondness for Burns spread to Scott and then to others and I have always had a deep love of lyric poetry. Shakespeare I was very late in forming an attachment for. This arose in part from the taste that I had formed for lyric poetry and rhymed verse in general (which I, like many another youth tried to imitate) and in part from an unfavorable impression gained from our early reading exercises in school.[12] In the Fourth and Fifth Readers of those days there were always preliminary exercises in voice culture and expression, which amounted to nothing in the absence of trained teachers but were a hateful nuisance to us pupils who had to grind our way perfunctorily through them. I remember particularly — "Hence! Home, you idle creatures. Get you home!" and how I hated it. If *that* was Shakespeare the less I had of it the better. So I always avoided it, and it was not until I was about twenty and had read Plutarch's *Julius Caesar*, and had become deeply absorbed in it, that I determined to see what Shakespeare's play was like. I have always been glad that I waited so long; for I doubt if under other circumstances it could have taken possession of me as it did. It was not long before I knew the play by heart. I remember the deep sadness of Pindarus' slaying of his master and his declaration immediately after — "Far from the country Pindarus will run where never Roman will take note of him." I was at this time away from home teaching school, and I had found it necessary to expend in dollars the (at that time) appalling sum of $71. Going home on a vacation I excited my mother's amusement by constantly humming over the above quotation from Shakespeare and winding it up with "Seventy-one dollars".

I also recall very vividly my first acquaintance with the mysteries of astronomy. In a little paper, the *Sunday School Herald*, which we took, there was a series of articles descriptive (in very simple and elementary terms) of the planets. They greatly excited my interest in the subject, but, so far as I could ascertain, there was not a book on astronomy in all the region round about; but finally I did get track of an old neglected book belonging to a neighbor (1½ miles away) by the name of Rich. I borrowed this book and read it nearly through on my way home (walking). Our teacher, Miss Alice Nourse, knew something about the constellations, and so I became quite familiar with the heavens, more so than I have ever been since so far as their visual appearance is concerned. I recall how I succeeded in following Venus (when a moving star) nearly the entire day, with the naked eye, and quite astonishing my schoolmates by being able to point it out to them as late as recess (about 11 A.M.).

I have often looked back with a feeling of regret that this beautiful receptiveness and enthusiasm in the acquisition of new knowledge, so characteristic of early youth, becomes somewhat blurred as one grows older. Surely no less wonderful was the later knowledge that showed me how to compute eclipses, latitude and longitude, etc., but it was so involved in a labyrinth of obstruse calculations that its beauty — the aroma of budding knowledge — was lacking. If one stops to think, he must admit that the working out, or discovery in practical form, of celestial physics, is almost as wonderful as the existence itself of those laws; yet it becomes prosaic — a matter of routine almost, to those engaged in such researches.

Other little incidents in my early reading and observations that have left something of an impression were the political campaigns of 1872 when the candidacy of Greeley made such a break in the Republican ranks (taking my father among others) and the interest I took in W. M. Evarts in the great Beecher trial of 1874, I believe.[13]

Like all boys, I was fond of all kinds of games, hunting, fishing and the like. In the small stream which ran through our farm there were a few fish, and very early in life my brother and I tried to catch them, but seldom succeeded. Trout rarely ventured into this stream, and all we could find were dace, suckers and shiners as we called them. In our first essays we used pin hooks — which reminds me of one of the stanzas in the little song, (*Rosy Nell*), that we used to sing:

> "The boys and girls would often go
> A-fishing in the brooks,
> With spools of thread for fishing lines
> And bended pins for hooks".

In those sports we rarely received parental encouragement. Father never indulged in them at all, and was so insistent on our constant application to work, that mother was generally rather reluctant to let us go. But still we went occasionally though we generally had to take those days when "it rained too hard to stay out of doors". But, as we shared the popular superstition that fish bite best in rainy weather, we did not look upon this choice of days as anything of a hardship.

Our chief fishing grounds were the Big Creek, to which I have already referred, and (Lime) Lake, a small pond about a square mile in area, situated near (Machias), $4\frac{1}{2}$ miles from home. I remember with great distinctness the catching of our first trout. One branch of Big Creek took its rise in a little marshy pond in the woods south of our house. Brother and I must have been quite small at this time and mother's reluctance to let us go alone into this dense forest and follow out a stream which we had never been on before, was quite natural. We had gotten a real fishhook somewhere, and a line, and having dug up some angle worms we set out. The tiny little rill gradually increased as we descended its course, but it was still a small stream — crystal clear — where we made our first venture. There was a little pool across which two moss covered logs were lying quite close together. We had such an impression of the wary qualities of the trout that we managed very carefully not to have them see us. We had not cut a fish pole or rod yet, and I took the line, crept up carefully on the logs and dropped the baited hook down between them. Sure enough, quick as a flash, a fine dark little trout, about four inches long, grabbed it. He was securely hooked and I pulled him out and went back to the shore trembling all over with a kind of "buck fever". It was our first success and a real one. We then cut us a fishing rod from the first suitable sapling, a "stringer" for the fish from a willow twig, or probably a birch, and went on our way rejoicing. After a long laborious day of it we reached Mr. Hall's sawmill, having met Uncle Frank on the way. We had caught eight fish in all. Then we went home, very proud, and mother cooked the fish, turning them in corn meal — a dish fit for kings.

Generally we had one excursion during the summer to (Lime) Lake. This was our only opportunity to get into a boat — nothing but row boats — and it had a proportionate effect upon our young imaginations. We were not allowed to go at first except in the company of some older neighbors. Perch and bass were the fish found in this lake and sometimes the fishing was very good. In somewhat later years, but still while we were quite young, my brother and I and two of our playmates went along; but had no success in fishing and finally went off on a sort of wild goose chase down the railroad to Yorkshire Center (now Delevan) some three miles away. Being very hungry and without money we fished up all the old iron we could find, plow points, bolts, etc. (the road had been recently built) and carried it to a hardware store where we sold it for a penny a pound and got us something to eat. I have often wondered what the merchant must have thought, and if he had no suspicions that the iron did not belong to us.

In our earlier life on the farm there were many opportunities for hunting but we had no gun. I still recall what vast flocks of pigeons used to pass north and south every year, but how their migrations ceased later. Black squirrels (a beautiful animal) were quite common and used to get into our corn fields a great deal. We often saw foxes and there were skunks, coons, a few mink and many rabbits. Clyde and I became enamored of trapping and we lived in its fullness, that intense thirst for game that led us to travel miles through the deep snow and set our traps here and there in hope of some definite result. But we were rarely successful, getting only a few skunk skins, a few squirrels, etc.

Finally, to make war on the great pest of our farms, the woodchuck, father procured an old army musket, a muzzle loading rifle, got the rifling bored out and thus converted it into a shotgun. The stunts I did with that cumbersome old weapon now seem really remarkable. It is a wonder that I never had an accident. In one season I killed over forty woodchucks besides much other small game. I even ran lead bullets and tried them in the smooth bore piece, but of course without results. Our work was so steady that I had but little time to hunt, frequently taking meal times for that purpose. I have always been fond of shooting though have never developed any special skill at it.

Another kind of hunting which I indulged in a very little was bee-tree hunting. The very idea was peculiarly fascinating and the scientific method was still more so. We used to take a little box with a sliding glass cover, put a little honey or sugar in it, go out into the fields, find a bee at work, carefully shake him into the box and close the cover before he could get out. So strong is the instinct of work in the little animal that its desire to improve the rare opportunity to secure a load of honey overcomes its alarm at captivity, and it almost invariably goes to work before the lid is opened. The box is taken to a convenient stump or post and after the bee has become thoroughly engaged in work the lid is softly opened. When the bee has secured its load it leaves the box just as it would have left the flower, ascends forty, fifty or a hundred feet in a spiral course until it gets its course and then starts in a "bee line" for its home wherever that may be. Notifying its co-workers it soon returns with one or more and after a time a regular transportation route is opened up, with bees coming and going all the time. The course of their flight having become definitely determined, the bee hunter seizes a time when the box contains two or three fresh arrivals, closes it and takes up a run in the direction that the bees have been following. He continues as long as he dares to without disturbing the bees too much, and then takes a new stand. After a while a new course is established and the process is repeated. If followed out long enough the home of the bees will surely be discovered. More often than not this will be in some domestic hive, but occasionally the hunter will be rewarded by finding a "bee tree", and he has a right to cut such a tree wherever found and take the honey therefrom.

Although I often tried this sport, and succeeded in establishing a course I was never successful in finding a "tree".

It was in [   ] that the first railroad came into our country, and up to that time I had never seen a locomotive.[14] I remember going to Delevan and watching the construction work where they were excavating a deep cut and making what seemed to me an enormously high fill in the valley of a branch of Cattaraugus Creek. Many years later I read in the life of Jacob Riis that he was working there at the time.[15] In the fall of this same year, the rails were laid in to our township and I well remember how Clyde and I one rainy day walked ten miles to Arcade to see a train, and also the impression it made on me. We then walked back to Delevan tired and worn out with the wind and rain and long tramp, but still borne up by the wonderful sights of the day. How big things look under the right conditions! Somewhat later, after regular train service was established I remember seeing a dapper little newsboy step off the train at our station, and watched him with envy and longed for the wonderful experiences that he must enjoy.

This railroad brought me my first actual experience with the outer world. Excursions to Niagara Falls became common and on one of these Clyde and I went, our parents generously remaining at home that we might go. It is all a dream now, as wonderful things generally are, and was too much mixed up with picnic features and rich food and resultant fatigue and headaches to have been of much benefit.

This brings up the matter of amusements and recreation of our lives in that country. In the summer there would always be a Sunday School picnic which was generally made quite an event. A long train of "dead-X" wagons was [   ] with seats fixed around the sides of the boxes and small evergreen "Christmas trees" fixed at intervals in these seats. There was more or less ornamentation and decoration in the form of flags and bunting, and there was always a *band!* This was usually made up of local talent and was simply a fife and drum band; but occasionally a genuine brass band was imported from some neighboring town, and that was a great treat. With all this array we would go off to some grove, generally four or five miles away, have some ceremonies on a stand prepared for the purpose, and then a dinner — the main event — composed of all the fine cooking that the neighborhood could command. It was a great day, generally, for fun, frolic, piece-speaking, and sick headaches — and [   ] afterward.

Another regular form of entertainment was the donation party given every winter to the minister who came to McKinstry Hollow to preach. These gatherings always took place in the evening. A usual feature of the feast always contributed on such occasions was oyster soup (which we never saw on any other occasion). The oysters were brought in little square corner oblong flat cans, and were prepared in a large clothes boiler from which the soup was distributed to the guests. After the dinner was over and the table cleared away the company resolved itself in a committee of the whole to play the various games prevalent in that part of the country. This always involved a great deal of kissing as a regular feature and has long since been frowned down upon, so far as my later knowledge goes. One of these games was "Swap and Catch-em", in which four persons (two men and two women) stood up in a square, holding each others arms strongly to brace against the rough handling they were subjected to, and around them a man would chase a woman (or *vice versa*) until he caught her when he would be entitled to a kiss (or compelled to take one whether he wanted it or not). Thereupon the person caught would take the place of one of the same sex in the square, the person catching would choose one from the company to chase her (or him) and so the fun would proceed by the hour.

Perhaps in another room a different sort of game would be going on. I remember one rather imperfectly in which quite a company of men and women, deposed alternately in a ring, holding each others hands, with one person in the center of the ring, would circle around singing a song something like this:

> King William was King James' son
> Of all the royal races run,
> Upon his breast he wore a star
> Pointing away to the compass far,
> Go choose to the east, go choose to the west,
> Go choose the one that you love best;

(Here the person inside the circle [   ] one of the opposite sex in the ring who promptly steps inside)

> Down on this carpet you must kneel,
> Sure as the grass grows in the field.
> Pledge your love in a kiss so sweet,
> Rise and stand upon your feet.

(Whereupon the person first in the circle retires to the ring and the mill goes to grinding again.)

It seems quite incredible now that these supremely silly games could so absorb a company, and I am glad to say that there was always an implacable element that could not stomach them; but the great majority kept at it until the small hours and considered it a good time.

While these things were going on the more weighty purpose of the "donation" was being carried out. The farmers (for they were all farmers) subscribed on a paper prepared for the purpose the amount they were willing to contribute to the support of the minister. These contributions were in cash and in "kind", that is, in potatoes or other produce such as was necessary for daily life. They seem now to have been very small — perhaps $50.00 or something like that; but everything was on a small scale then, and small things seemed large to us.

There was, of course, the annual circus to some of the neighboring villages, but we were rarely allowed to go. There were also occasional dances, but these were not a part of our "permissibles". Going with the girls had a sort of stilted, stiff formality about it that seems quite out of keeping with the free life of the country. It was a matter of vast rivalry both among boys and girls and was the chief feature of the many revival and other meetings we used to have (that is, the chief feature of the young folks). It seemed to be considered necessary for every girl to have a boy take her home (except with some few parents who insisted on taking their own girls home). After the meeting (or whatever it was) was over, the boys would line up in the entry way to the school house, opposite the main exit, and waited for the girls to appear from the other side of the entry way. When a boy espied his girl, he would walk up to her bravely, extend his bended elbow and offer, in some set formula, to see her home. It was a rather trying minute for the boys were always afraid of getting the "mitten" and becoming the butt of raillery on the part of their acquaintances. It was a curious performance. The idea of escorting the girls home was not based at all upon the necessity for such an escort, for girls were safe in that country, but it was simply a scheme to establish relations of standing with one's favorite girl which the rest of the community would understand. Then, of course, there were often genuine attachments and these walks meant a great deal; but on the whole the social relations of young men and women were quite different from what I have observed since. Perhaps judging from my own recollections, there was a greater distance between boys and girls than is evident in modern society — more stiffness and less meeting on common ground, perhaps, for that very reason attachments were stronger; at any rate they were strong enough.

It seems to me, as I look back, that our variety of boyhood games was less than boys now enjoy. Baseball, though very attractive to me, was still very far from the modern scientific game. Football I never saw until I went to Cornell. Pom-pom-pull-away (if that is the way to spell it), Duck-on-the-Rock were games of a simple character that we played a great deal. Gould was per —

January 1, 1917

It is now nearly nine years since I began these memoirs. One thing and another has arisen to prevent its continuance and completion. My health has steadily continued to decline until now it seems that, if I am ever going to complete the work, I had better be about it. I see I left off rather abruptly, apparently in the middle of a sentence[16]

A Chittenden Checklist

The following checklist includes only those items important to Western history. Of the great number of reports and articles written on professional engineering subjects, only those which pertain to the West are included.

BOOKS

The Yellowstone National Park: Historical and Descriptive. Cincinnati, 1895

American Fur Trade of the Far West: A History of the Pioneer Trading Posts and Early Fur Companies of the Missouri Valley and Rocky Mountains and of the Overland Commerce with Santa Fe. 3 Vols. New York, 1902

History of Early Steamboat Navigation on the Missouri: Life and Adventures of Joseph La Barge, Pioneer Navigator and Indian Trader. 2 Vols. New York, 1903.

Life, Letters and Travels of Father Pierre-Jean De Smet, S.J., 1801-1873. In collaboration with A. T. Richardson. 4 Vols. New York, 1904, 1905.

War or Peace: A Present Duty and a Future Hope. Chicago, 1911.

Verse. Privately published for Christmas distribution. Seattle, 1916.

ARTICLES AND REPORTS

"The Ancient Town of Fort Benton in Montana." *Magazine of American History* XXIV (December, 1890), 409-25.

"List of Steamboat Wrecks on the Missouri River from the Beginning of Steamboat Navigation to the Present Time." Being a part of Appendix W W of the Annual Report of the Chief of Engineers for 1897. Washington, 1897.

"Report on System of Tourist Routes in Yellowstone Park." *Annual Report of the Chief of Engineers, 1903.* Washington, D.C., 1903. Pp. 2444-77.

"Report on Boundaries and Other Matters Pertaining to Yosemite National

Park, 1904." *Commission Report*, Department of the Interior, Washington, D.C., 1904.

"Report on Flood Control of the Sacramento River, 1904." *Annual Report of Commissioner of Public Works for 1905*. Sacramento, California, 1905.

"Report on Floods in the Duwamish and Puyallup Rivers, Washington: King and Pierce Counties." Seattle, 1907.

"Report on Forests and Reservoirs in Their Relation to Stream Flow." *Transactions* of American Society of Civil Engineers, Vol. 62 (1909), Pp. 245-346.

"The Puget Sound and Inland Empire Railway; Cascade Tunnel Route." 1909, Seattle. (The paper on the Cascade Tunnel Route was published under the pseudonym Itothe Phucher — "Eye to the Future").

"Report of the Water Supply of San Francisco." Spring Valley Water Company, San Francisco, 1912.

"Ports of the Pacific." *Transactions* of American Society of Civil Engineers, Vol. 76 (1913), 155-240.

"Notes on Flood Control." *Transactions* of American Society of Civil Engineers, Vol. 79 (1915), 110-253. Reprinted as *House Document* No. 2, 64th Congress, 1st Session.

"A Northern Railroad Entrance to Seattle." *Proceedings*, Pacific Northwest Society of Engineers, XIII (1914), 3-7.

UNPUBLISHED MANUSCRIPTS

(Chittenden seldom dated his unpublished manuscripts. However, when he did so, the date is included in the citation.)

"Journal of a Trip to the Pacific Coast." First entry is December 9, 1896; last entry is dated January 8, 1896, but this should read 1897.

"Journal of a Trip to Wyoming and Colorado in May 1897." Trip started from St. Louis on April 30 and ended May 17, 1897.

"Trip of August 1897." From St. Louis August 2 to September 11 (though Chittenden mistakenly entered August 11). Chittenden visited the Jackson Hole country.

Diaries: Six diaries run chronologically from November 1878 to February 1912 with only the years 1900-1902 missing.

"Notes on the Reservoir Service." No date given. Reminiscences of experiences in flood control of the Missouri River.

"Notes for History of Steamboating on Missouri River." No date, but written at Sioux City. This contains notes, chapter organization, etc., of what probably was the first manuscript of his *History of Early Steamboat Navigation on the Missouri River.*

"Lake Washington Canal." Notes compiled 1906. Includes charts, graphs, statistics, estimates concerning the building of the Lake Washington Ship Canal and the Government Locks.

"Personal Notes." Seattle, 1908. About 60 closely written pages of the beginning of an autobiography, never finished.

"Historical Work." Typescript. September, 1917. 4 pages.

"The Yellowstone." Typescript. September, 1917. 8 pages.

"The Harbor Island Episode: A History." Typescript. Seattle, 1915.

Footnotes

I. BIOGRAPHICAL NOTES

1 Chittenden papers: Typescript of remarks of Judge C. H. Hanford at Glacier National Park in 1925. Chittenden Papers, Washington State Historical Society.

2 Chittenden-United Nations of the World correspondence, Washington State Historical Society.

3 *The American Fur Trade of the Far West: A History of the Pioneering Trading Posts and Early Fur Companies of the Missouri Valley and the Rocky Mountains and of the Overland Commerce with Santa Fe.* 3 Vols. New York, 1902.

4 *Life, Letters and Travels of Father Pierre-Jean De Smet.* In collaboration with A. T. Richardson. 4 Vols. New York, 1905.

5 *History of Early Steamboat Navigation on the Missouri: Life and Adventures of Joseph La Barge, Pioneer Navigator and Indian Trader.* 2 Vols. New York, 1903.

6 *The Yellowstone National Park: Historical and Descriptive.* Cincinnati, 1895.

7 *War or Peace: A Present Duty and a Future Hope.* Chicago, 1911.

8 Chittenden was frequently asked to contribute articles on many questions of national significance. Most of these pieces were unrelated to his historical researches, having to do with his position on the great questions of American participation in international affairs.

9 Chittenden papers: Chittenden-Norman Angell correspondence, Washington State Historical Society.

10 Chittenden papers: Chittenden-David Starr Jordan correspondence, Washington State Historical Society.

11 Chittenden papers: Washington State Historical Society collections.

12 Turner, Frederick Jackson: *Rise of the New West*, preface, p. 28.

13 Billington, Ray: *Westward Expansion*, p. 807.

14 Nute, Grace Lee: Introduction, *A History of the American Fur Trade of the Far West*, Stanford, Cal. 1954, pp. viii.

15 DeVoto, Bernard: *Across the Wide Missouri*, pp. xii.

16 *Historical Work*, Chapter V, this book.

17 Ibid.

18 Ibid.

19 See Appendix to Chapter V, Footnote 1.

20 See Cullum's *Biographical Register of Graduates of the U. S. Military Academy*, Serial No. 3023.

21 See Chapter II: *Editor's Notes*.

22 Public Law 779, 84th Congress, Second Session. A telegram to Major General James B. Cress July 24, 1956 states as follows: "H. R. 7943 Signed by President this afternoon—Stewart Bragdon."

23 Under the pseudonym, Itothe Phucher ("Eye To The Future") Chittenden proposed a great Cascade Tunnel which would link eastern and western Washington with an all-weather road. He was ridiculed for this visionary proposal, but the Washington Legislature, in its 1961 Session, appropriated moneys to begin this great project, with the tunnel to go through the Naches Pass.

24 Chittenden papers: Letter from C. W. Smith, Librarian, University of Washington, dated September 12, 1925, to Mrs. Nettie M. Chittenden (the General's widow) lists the Chittenden items donated by Mrs. Chittenden to the University of Washington Library. The list includes copies of three Chittenden books, nine unbound magazine articles, ten unpublished manuscripts, two manuscript letters, three pamphlets, and a bundle of newspaper clippings. Most of the items, except for the magazine articles, are duplicated in the Chittenden collection at the Washington State Historical Society.

25 The records here referred to are the business records of the American Fur Company.

26 Cress, Mrs. Eleanor Chittenden: her manuscript note at the end of the typescript of Chittenden's notes on the Yellowstone.

27 Chittenden papers: William Howard Taft-Chittenden correspondence,

Washington State Historical Society.

28 *Seattle Times:* Obituary notice, October 18, 1917.

II. THE YELLOWSTONE

Editor's Notes

1 Chittenden papers: Biography as submitted to *National Cyclopedia of American Biography*, Vol. XVII, page 404, number 16.

2 Ibid.

3 Chittenden papers, Washington State Historical Society.

4 Eleanor Cress-Bruce Le Roy correspondence, Washington State Historical Society.

5 See page 24 ff.

6 See page 119, Appendix to Chapter III.

Chittenden's Text

1 According to Theodore P. Chittenden, this European trip was a kind of delayed honeymoon taken by his father and mother in 1891. Only a passing reference to this trip appears in the Chittenden papers.

2 Cullum's *Biographical Register of Graduates of the U. S. Military Academy*, Serial No. 3023.

3 His reputation for work in the Yellowstone was firmly established by virtue of his achievements during the first assignment from 1891 to 1893. The second assignment to the Park came in 1899 at the close of service in the Spanish-American War during which he had served as Chief Engineer of the Fourth Army Corps, with a temporary rank of Lt. Colonel of Volunteers. His second Yellowstone assignment lasted from 1899 to 1906.

4 The way Chittenden tackled the wilderness, armed only with "hand level and strong stick" plus a little hardtack and a fisherman's optimism as to where the next meal was coming from, is strongly reminiscent of the philosophy of Major A. B. Rogers, who in the same decade, surveyed and explored the Selkirks and the Rockies for Jim Hill, the "Empire Builder", while laying out the transcontinental routes of the Canadian Pacific and Great Northern railways.

5 See Appendix to Chapter V, footnote 1.

6 See illustration of "The Golden Gate Viaduct" on page 35.

7 See Editor's Notes to Chapter II.

8 See Appendix to Chapter V, footnote 1. *The Yellowstone National Park* is still in print, available from Stanford University Press.

III. JOURNALS OF WESTERN TRIPS

Journal of Trip to Pacific Coast, December 9, 1896 — January 8, 1897

1 Having completed a two year assignment as Executive Officer of a Board of Engineers in charge of a canal survey between Lake Erie and the Ohio River, Chittenden was appointed in 1896 Secretary of the Missouri River Commission, in personal charge of the improvement of the Osage and Gasconade Rivers in Missouri, the Surveys on the Missouri River, and later to conduct surveys for reservoir sites in Wyoming and Colorado.

2 The famous "Cross of Gold" speech by William Jennings Bryan which electrified the country and dramatized the national controversy over the question of whether the United States would permit free and unlimited coinage of silver at a ratio of sixteen to one, or would maintain the gold standard advocated by the Republicans under William McKinley. Bryan and "free silver" were defeated in the election of 1896.

3 Before his appointment to West Point in 1880 and following a few months at Cornell University, Chittenden taught school for several months in Cuba, New York. See Chittenden diaries, Chittenden collection, Washington State Historical Society.

4 Federal control of western land irrigation resulted in part from the demands of just such professional groups. Later, in 1908 the federal government, under the conservation-minded Theodore Roosevelt, launched a full-scale movement to conserve natural resources. President Roosevelt, in that year, called the first conference of governors for an inventory of the nation's natural resources. This resulted in the establishment of conservation units of government in certain states and in the improvement of existing agencies in others. These state agencies have, in the course of time, become a powerful element of effective cooperation with federal conservation agencies.

In notes for a biography prepared for the *National Cyclopedia of American Biography* Chittenden refers to a paper he prepared on the influence of forests upon stream flow. He says, "It was at the height of the forestry propaganda under the Pinchot regime. The press of the country was full of material furnished by the Forestry Bureau. The lecture platform was the scene of innumerable addresses inspired from the same source. Photographers scoured the country to get pictures of denuded hillsides, river sandbars, flooded valleys — all the result of deforestation. Never in all history has there been such an exhibition of unscientific propaganda, such a violation of the principles of common sense. The movement was a carefully worked-out scheme to take the Rivers and Harbors works of the country out of the hands of the Corps of Engineers. Following the debacle of Captain Carter ten years before, the Corps had steadily lost ground with the public and at this time, or shortly before, was at the lowest ebb of its prestige since its history as a separate organization began . . . it so happened that my professional work had brought to my attention in a practical way this relation between forest and stream flow. For many years I had had to open up the roads in the Yellowstone, a densely forested country, in the season of floods. I then learned that the floods of that and similar regions *came from the forests*, not from the open country. Upon investigation I found the cause, and was led by this aspect of the forestry theory in one case, to investigate it in others. I studied with particular care the experience of Europe, and finally became fully convinced that the conventional forest theory — as elaborated by Pinchot, had nothing to support it. In the midst of the unparalleled success of his propaganda, and contrary to the advice of a veteran officer of my own Corps, who feared that I would do more harm than good, I prepared, during the summer of 1907, an elaborate paper which was presented to the American Society of Civil Engineers, and by it published for discussion in the Proceedings." (Report on Forests and Reservoirs in Their Relation to Stream Flow. *Transactions of American Society of Civil Engineers*, Vol. 62 [1909], 245-346).

The effect was instantaneous. There was, as a matter of fact, a strong undercurrent of feeling that the forest propaganda was being carried to ridiculous extremes utterly in defiance of scientific data. To all this element, the paper, based on scientific data and analysis, was most welcome; for it gave something definite to stand upon. To the ultra-forestry advocates it was the most marvelous thing imaginable. It came like a thunderbolt (next few words illegible). Mr. Pinchot and Mr. [   ] went to New York when the paper was presented and opposed it in the most vigorous terms. When Congress met, President Roosevelt in his last annual message, rebuked the paper and its author (without directly mentioning either) in his usual emphatic manner. But these efforts had exactly the opposite effect. They called public attention, in Congress particularly, to the paper and secured for it a publicity which would have taken a long while to secure without it. The paper was published in full in the Congressional Record. Over twenty engineers throughout the country sent in written discussions, and these, with the original paper and the author's rebuttal made a total of over 300 pages, with an exhaustive array of data, illustrations, etc. Nearly all the discussions, except those fostered by the Pinchot following of five or six, were either outspoken in support of the author's views or at least friendly to them. One, George F. Swain, who had been asked to prepare an answer to the paper, took a distinctly antagonistic ground."

Chittenden then went on to state that the effect of the paper upon the public attitude toward the Corps of Engineers was highly favorable, and the work of the Corps in building the Panama Canal (then under way) completely restored public confidence in the Corps; that he regarded this paper and his "Reservoir Report" as the two most important in his professional engineering career.

In justice to Theodore Roosevelt and to the massive accomplishments of his administration in the field of conservation it must be remarked that his signing of the Reclamation Act in 1902 and the successful completion of irrigation projects in ten western states during his administration indicated a difference in approach rather than a failure of vision.

5 Mr. Schuyler was correct. The acorns in the tree were planted (or deposited, a better word, in this case) by the California woodpecker, creating what is popularly termed a "nut bank", a natural phenomenon still to be seen in that part of California which Chittenden was visiting.

6 San Pedro and the people of California won.

Journal of Trip to Wyoming and Colorado, May 1897.

1 See the *American Fur Trade of the Far West*, Vol. I, p. 473-474. Chittenden must have elaborated upon this description of Devil's Gate, the Valley of the Sweetwater, the Astorians, and the conjecture about the buffalo, basing the account closely on this entry in his journal. In two or three instances, the sentences are nearly identical.

2 Chittenden devoted Chapter 26 of *The American Fur Trade of the Far West* to the Oregon Trail. What impression the Trail created on famous travellers interested him greatly. Father De Smet, Chittenden observed, considered the Oregon Trail one of the finest highways in the world, telling of the amazing impact the Trail made on Indians who viewed it for the first time:

"They conceived a high idea of the countless WHITE Nation, as they express it. They fancied that all had gone over that road,

and that an immense void must exist in the land of the rising sun
. . . they styled the route the Great Medicine Road of the Whites".

Journal of Trip to Jackson Hole and Idaho, August 2 — September 11, 1897.

1 The author cites Fort John and Fort Laramie in several places in his fur
trade history. Fort John, the trading post for the American Fur Company, was described by Dr. F. A. Wislizenus (in *A Journey to the Rocky
Mountains in the Year 1839*) as being rectangular in shape, eighty by
one hundred feet, with flanking towers on three sides and a very strong
gate. Fort Laramie, the military post, stood about a mile farther
upstream.

2 Chittenden really meant Fort McKenzie which was located near the
present site of Sheridan, Wyoming. Fort McKenzie, named for Kenneth
McKenzie, a president of the Columbia Fur Company, was constructed
in 1832. It was the scene of a battle with the Blackfeet on August 28,
1833. At the time of the battle, Prince Maximilian with the artist,
Charles Bodmer, was in the post. Both left sketches of the battle and
Maximilian gave us an exciting narrative of the event in his *Travels
in the Interior of North America.*

3 The Battle of the Little Big Horn.

4 Jackson Hole, named after David Jackson, an associate of William Sublette. Jackson, in the winter of 1828-29, used the present site of Jackson
Hole as a base for fur-trading operations along the Snake River where
it flows near the Teton Range.

5 Parley Pratt, one of Joseph Smith's original Council of Twelve, was
appointed one of the Twelve Apostles at Kirtland, Ohio in 1835. Pratt
continued to hold his high place in the Church until he was murdered
in 1857.

IV. NOTES ON THE RESERVOIR SERVICE

1 Annual Report of the Chief of Engineers for 1897. See Appendix D. This
section of the official report was prepared by Chittenden, then a Captain
of Engineers, USA, and Secretary of the Missouri River Commission.
For this Appendix Chittenden compiled a list of the steamboat wrecks
on the Missouri River, a project which led directly to his *History of
Early Steamboat Navigation on the Missouri River*. The Appendix
was also published separately. Copies in South Dakota and Washington
State Historical Society collections.

2 Chittenden's attendance at the Irrigation Congress at Phoenix resulted from tours of inspection to numerous reservoir sites in the West. His report was printed by Congress as House Document 141, 56th Congress, 2nd Session, and was reprinted in part in the *Congressional Record.* Containing a strong recommendation for government aid in irrigation work, particularly regarding water storage, the report became very popular throughout the West.

3 Chittenden's claim about "the only survey ever made" cannot be confirmed.

4 See Chapter III, *Journal of Trip to Jackson Hole and Idaho.*

5 See Chittenden: *The Yellowstone National Park*, page 272:
"Near the eighth mile-post, where an old freight road branches off to the Canyon Hotel, is the site of the hold-up of 1897. At this point a few masked highwaymen stopped all the regular coaches of the day, including a government conveyance with an army officer and his family. No bodily injury was done anyone, but the pockets of the entire party were successfully emptied of all valuables. The exploit was a very clever piece of work."

6 In a report prepared for the *National Cyclopedia of American Biography* Chittenden said: "The author regards this paper and his reservoir report . . . as the two most important facts in his professional (engineering) career".

V. HISTORICAL WORK

Editor's Notes

1 *A Guide to the Study of the United States of America*, Washington, D.C., 1960. P. 510.

Chittenden's Text

1 The first edition of *The Yellowstone National Park* was published in 1895 by Stewart and Kidd Company, Cincinnati. In the Preface to the first edition Chittenden states that the book grew out of an Army assignment to the Park in 1891-1892, and a second assignment returning him to Yellowstone from 1899-1906, following service in the Spanish-American War. Successive editions of the book incorporated important revisions. The 1915 edition, for example, contained an expansion of the narratives concerning Jim Bridger and John Colter. The book was revised

by the author once more shortly before his death in 1917. Posthumous editions of the book have been revised and updated by his daughter, Eleanor Chittenden Cress. *The Yellowstone National Park,* adopted many times as the official guidebook to the Park, is still available under the Stanford University Press imprint.

2 Chittenden said that writing the history of the fur trade took six years, being sandwiched in between official duties with the Missouri River Commission. The period of that assignment spent in St. Louis gave time and access to the records of the American Fur Company. He was one of the first to employ business records as source material for writing history.

3 Chittenden was wrong. Grace Lee Nute prepared an excellent calendar of the American Fur Company papers, published by The American Historical Association. Nonetheless, it was a heroic task they both performed.

4 A large scrapbook of clippings of contemporary reviews in the Washington State Historical Society collection bears the author out. None were adverse. Most of the reviews appeared in newspapers and popular journals. Chittenden's acceptance by the academic historian came at a later date. Though his work is customarily cited in all good fur-trade bibliographies today, the academic historian generally observes that Chittenden pioneered the work, marking a path for later, more specific treatments of different segments of fur trade history. Billington, for example, in the 1950 edition of *The Western Frontier, 1830-1860,* says, "Chittenden's neglect of the southwestern trade is corrected in Cleland's *This Reckless Breed of Men: The Trappers and Fur Traders of the Southwest*". Long before this, in the Press of the Pioneers Edition of *The American Fur Trade of the Far West,* Stallo Vinton, the editor, added a fine short account of American Fur Company activities in the Southwest, together with a bibliography.

5 Chittenden was right, the book still sells. Most recent edition was published by Academic Reprints, Stanford, California (not to be confused with Stanford Press).

6 The author's conceptual approach to the opening of the American West finds interesting parallel in Bernard De Voto's frontier thesis. Both writers came to see that the Missouri River, that great highway of explorer and fur trader, was, in itself, the "Course of Empire", and the fabled Northwest Passage. The Missouri River, for both writers, was the "key" to the westward movement.

Letters from contemporary historians followed in the wake of publication of Chittenden's Books.

A letter from Reverend L. B. Palladino, S. J., Missoula, Montana, Oct. 12, 1910.

In a letter, dated Sioux City, Iowa, January 26, 1904, and before me — having kept it, anticipating how serviceable it might eventually prove — you were kind enough to inform me that you had evidence indicating quite conclusively that the Indian deputation of 1831, was not from the Flatheads of the Bitter Root Valley at all, but from the Nez Perce. As I am actually engaged in preparing a new and revised edition of "Indian and White in the Northwest" I should prize it indeed as a most special favor, if I could be helped by such evidence as you possess toward correcting any error of mine on that point.

I have been much interested in "Life, Letters and Travels of Father De Smet", brought out jointly by yourself and A. T. Richardson, whom I have had the pleasure of meeting in North Yakima, Washington, where I spent the last two years. I cannot help tendering you and Mr. Richardson my congratulations on the merits and excellence of your joint production. My appreciation, I know, does not count much, but you may rest assured that it is true, as its expression is sincere and hearty.

Yours, truly and respectfully,

L. B. Palladino, S. J.

A letter from W. F. Wagner, 501 L Street, N.W., Washington, D.C. Jan. 10, 1912 to: Brig. Gen. H. M. Chittenden, Seattle, Wash.

I have recently come across a little historical data which I am sure will interest you, the original Will of John Day which is in the hands of Alexander MacKenzie, who secured it from the MacKenzie family, sons of Donald in Chautauqua Co., N.Y., where it was probated about 1836 or 8. I have been in correspondence with one of the sons of Donald some four years but they are of a rather peculiar trend and could get but little with reference to the father's adventures in the West, three of the family have died in the last three years, but one or two still remain. Alexander the above mentioned is the grandson of Roderic, and grand-nephew of Donald, he is interested in historical data along these lines and secured the above from his relatives at Mayville, he has but recently sent me a copy of its contents, which I have sent to the Missouri Hist. Society.*

He was born in Culpepper, Va., it gives fathers and mothers names, and mentions two brothers but not by name. It was drawn in the presence of Donald MacKenzie on the 19th of Feb. 1819, and he died the following day, according to an added note and witnessed in the presence of D. MacK. The money due him from Astor he willed to Rachel daughter of D. Mac-Kenzie of the Columbia River, which shows that the latter had probably an Indian family on the Columbia, he also had some lands near St. Louis by a Spanish grant adjoining those of Mon. Chouteau, as well as an interest in some mines all of which he disposes of by the above will. The executor was compelled to bring an action against Astor to collect the amount due, which was paid with interest about 1838. It is witnessed by well known characters of the then fur trade.

This at least settles the time of his death and that it was not at Astoria, as given by Irving, and rather supports Ross. He was no doubt one of the company of Donald MacK. who were trapping in the Snake river country, as more fully described by Ross in his "Fur Hunters". I trust you are well and that now as you are retired you will have more time to devote to historical matters, to whose pages you have contributed so brilliantly. I beg to remain,

Very respectfully,

W. F. Wagner

*

The John Day Will and Testament and a letter to W. F. Wagner from Mary Louise Dalton, of St. Louis, are printed in full on pp. 184-187 in *Donald MacKenzie: King of the Northwest*, by Cecil W. MacKenzie, Los Angeles, 1937.

Another letter from W. F. Wagner, Jan. 30th 1912.

In reply to your letter of Jan. 23rd, I will say with reference to the time and place of the death of John Day, we have two accounts, which are at variance. In "Astoria" and "Ross Fur Hunters". In the latter he states, if my memory serves me right, that he died on a certain river a branch of the Snake about 1819. Ross himself was conducting operations in this country some years later when, he makes this statement, he probably being near the place at the time, you may get the exact data by referring to his work which I have not at hand at present.

We have therefore two adverse statements of facts, both of which are entitled to credit, in the absence of supplemental evidence.

We have not, however, to my knowledge, anything other than this statement in Astoria, of the time and place of his death, with which to verify the same.

The Will which cannot be questioned, as it distributed his estate and the executor by its authority collected what was due him from Astor, which Astor certainly would have questioned had it been drawn 8 years after his (Days) death. This Will was drawn on Feb. 19th 1819 so as to time at least "Astoria" is wrong. It also states that he died on the 20th giving the hour in the PRESENCE of Donald MacKenzie his Executor.

WHERE WAS DONALD MACKENZIE ON FEBRUARY 20TH 1819? (I think it will be admitted that he was not at Astoria or Fort George.)

Again turning to Ross, if my memory is correct, he is on one of his numerous trapping expeditions, with his motley troop of trappers in the Snake River country, which I think at this time left Fort Nez Perce near the mouth of the Snake in the fall and remained in the trapping country during the season, all of which is in support of the Ross statement.

My notes on the Will does not make mention of the exact place and it is a question if the place could have been designated, except in a general way, in this then almost unknown wilderness. A true copy of the Will may be more full on this point.

That "Astoria" is wrong in point of time by 7 or 8 years there can be no question — and this would carry with it the presumption that it is equally as liable to error in the same event as to place, they usually go hand in hand — besides the time of his death is not within the period and scope of Astoria history.

Day was from Culpepper, Va., near here, it mentions his father, mother and two brothers, who so far as he knew were living at the time of his death.

The money due him from Astor he willed to Rachel MacKenzie who was a daughter of Donald by an Indian mother.

I have recently had a letter from Judge Douglas of St. Louis who states that he has the promise of the MS journal of Wilson Price Hunt for the Mo. Hist. Soc'y. which may disclose the source of Irving's information in Astorian events to some extent at least should such be the case. I will get a copy of the journal, or should it contain anything of importance relative to Western History.

I am,

Very respectfully,

W. F. Wagner

A letter from Reverend J. Neilson Barry, Rector, St. Stephen's Parish,

Baker, Oregon, to: "Gen. H. M. Chittenden, Seattle, Wash. — December 21, 1911".

I have succeeded in obtaining copies of your most interesting work, and I am delighted with it, as it contains just the information I have been desiring.

For some time I have been working out the route of Hunt's party through this locality, your data entirely agrees with my conclusions — the map of early routes published by the Government, Prof. Lyman's Columbia River and Holman's Oregon Counties in the Oregon Quarterly put the route through Wallowa Country.

We are to have a centennial celebration of the arrival of the first white man in Baker Valley Thursday Dec. 28th. Mr. T. C. Elliott of Walla Walla, Mr. Geo. H. Himes of the Oregon Historical Society, Maj. Lee Morehouse and Judge S. A. Lowell of Pendleton are to come and possibly Prof. Lyman of Whitman College. If it were possible for you to be present also, Baker would be greatly honored, and it would be a real delight for me to meet you.

We are to visit the "fountain" mentioned by Ogden in his journals, which is five miles up the river, I succeeded in locating it last summer, and it showed the trail of the Hudson's Bay trappers across the divide between Powder and Burnt Rivers, along Beaver Creek, this route abounded in beavers which have still continued until recent years, and the "fountain" was the natural parting of the trails to the headwaters of the Malheur, the old Nevada road to Silver City turned off there. It was not adapted to wheels down Burnt River, so the wagon trail left Burnt River further down and crossed the divide to Powder Valley by Virtue Flat. Sutton Creek along which the railroad runs is between these two routes, and undoubtedly Hunt came along that Sutton Creek route, as the description shows, and so must have encamped where Baker now stands — there is black sand resembling gunpowder in that locality — the only place where I have been able to find it, and it may have suggested the name "Powder" River.

Do you know the meaning of "Portpellah" or "Takinpa" the names given to the Powder and North Powder on the Lewis and Clark map?

Rev. C. G. Edwards of Blackfoot, Idaho, who discovered the site of Fort Hall and who represented the Governor of Idaho at the Astoria Centennial has been endeavoring to find the site of Fort Henry and asked me for help — I have sent him all the data I knew, but last night I found in your work just what he desired, and hope soon to hear that he has located the spot.

I am certainly glad that you wrote what you did in regard to Bancroft and Irving. It was wholly unjust and apparently he had never read the preface mentioning Franchere's Narrative — and to abuse Bonneville because his men killed those Indians was utterly unjust.

I am endeavoring to locate Bonneville's route over the Wallowa Mountains and have printed a series of extracts in a local paper in that region, and considerable interest has been aroused. The valley which Irving supposed was Grande Ronde which Bonneville visited shortly after the "digger" Indian had left him, and just before he crossed the Wallowa Mountains the first time, was evidently Pine Valley.

"Woodville" Creek mentioned in Astoria in Stuart's return journey when he reached the Snake is evidently Burnt River. It seems to be called "Flint" on the Lewis and Clark map. But I cannot make out whether Gun Creek mentioned in Bonneville is that river or Malheur, do you know?

I have had several series of extracts from Astoria published, and for the past month have had the events of each day in the newspaper, which is doing much to create interest, resulting in over eighty men planning to attend the banquet given to the speakers next Thursday.

I had noticed the same thing which you mentioned in regard to Irving's dates — oddly enough the one time when he seemed at fault was this same day a century ago (Dec. 21, 1811) when he seemed to skip Dec. 22 — yet in working out the events for the daily item in the paper, it seemed clear that the events covered two days, as they probably went as far down the Snake as Old's Ferry before deciding to sacrifice a horse.

The Handbook of American Indians (Bureau Am. Eth., Bul. 30.) under the heading of Arikara Indians mentions their custom of using a canoe made up of buffalo skin, which was evidently copied by Hunt's party in crossing the Snake. Vol. 1. p. 85.

Putnam's Son's are about to publish a student's edition of Astoria, and have asked me to write a chapter in regard to Hunt's route — as my studies have been westward from Fort Henry your valuable books give exactly the information I have been needing — I find some slight differences, and a number of places I can not locate.

Chapter XXVI. Paragraph 8 says of the Black Hills "Baffled in his attempts to traverse this mountain chain Mr. Hunt skirted along it to the SOUTHWEST keeping it on his RIGHT." Was it the Powder River Range? or some other range, or has Irving mixed something?

I have been trying to locate the Peak of the Big Horn they saw Aug. 17th and wrote to the Postmaster at Gillette, but she seems to confuse that range with the Rocky Mountains. Cloud Peak seems to be the highest point but is too far north for their route.

On p. 197 you use the word "northeast" in describing the location of Pumpkin Creek and Powder River, is that a misprint or is my map wrong? It locates Pumpkin Butte in the Southwest corner of Weston Co.

Your books says (p. 197) "crossing the river it reaches the base of the mountains along one of the southernmost branches of Crazy Woman's Fork of Powder River". Astoria Chap. XXVII Paragraph 4 speaks of going 18 miles up the River, so it would seem as though they followed up the Powder to Nine Mile Creek, and up that Westward toward the Big Horn.

I had located Caldron Linn at Shoshone Falls — Stuart on his return East Chapter XLIV was at Salmon Falls Aug. 25th and reached Caldron Linn Aug. 29th—. If the present Salmon Falls is the same place, and also the place where Hunt found Indian encampment shortly after leaving Caldron Linn, it would seem to agree with that identification. Hunt surely lost sense of distance when he traveled by water.

I had supposed that Hunt left the Snake about due south of Boise rather than Henry's Ferry, as it makes it a less distance to the Boise River and the Snake was evidently flowing northward at the point where they left it, as Irving speaks of it "still running to the north" when they descended the Boise to its junction with the Snake.

Your work is a real delight to me and I anticipate many pleasant hours in company with it — I do hope that the author will be able to attend our Centennial Dec. 28, we will give you a cordial welcome.

Very sincerely yours,

J. Neilson Barry

VI. PERSONAL NOTES

1 The "essays, maps, diaries, etc.," referred to are in the Chittenden collection at the Washington State Historical Society (see Chittenden Checklist, Appendix A). A few notable exceptions were the papers distributed to several institutions a few months prior to his death in 1917. The historical societies of Missouri, South Dakota and Montana received some of the materials which Chittenden used in preparing the history of the fur trade. His "Notes on the Astorians", for example, he presented to South Dakota; an original letter of Pierre Menard he gave to Montana; to the Missouri Historical Society went a "Log book of the American Fur Company, 1840-50," and a number of photographs of people and views significant to fur trade history.

When Chittenden refers to "throwing away a great deal of accumulated rubbish" we can only hope that the author's lifelong sense of historical value was operative. His memoirs refer to a considerable file of correspondence with Dr. Elliott Coues, for example, no trace of which has been located. We also wonder what became of a lengthy correspondence with Frances Fuller Victor, woman historian of the fur trade and the "River of the West".

2 Picture of the Chittenden home is not reproduced, but is in the collection of the Washington State Historical Society.

3 Though the author never mentions the fact, Cattaraugus County, the setting for his memoirs of youth, was, in itself, a historic locale. Schoolcraft, the Indian authority, once likened Cattaraugus' succession of hills and valleys to "a piece of rumpled calico". Here once lived a prehistoric, mound-building people before the Senecas, one of the Iroquois Nation, came to drive out the Eries, and in turn, were driven out by the white man. The county still abounds in Indian names, streams like the Conewango and the Tunegawant and places like Kill Buck, Ischua and Gowanda. Cattaraugus County is part of the three-million acre tract that the shrewd Dutch capitalists, who formed the Holland Land Company, bought from Robert Morris in 1793. The Company was established on March 11, 1808. Olean was the mother town, Ellicottville was the county seat until 1868 when Little Valley replaced it. Certain actions in the French and Indian War and the Revolution occurred in Cattaraugus County.

4 The author's sense of geographical direction proved useful in his studies of the westward movement. Chittenden's concept of the importance of historical geography is clearly borne out in the biographical memoir, a distinct "sense of place" informing the entire narrative.

5 The historian never mentions the influence of the canals in western New York history. True, the great era of the "canallers" was over, having reached its peak by mid-nineteenth century, when it was superseded by the coming of the railroads. Even so, the rivers of Cattaraugus County were used by flat boats and barges to link up with Erie Canal traffic. Because the Canal was thirty-five miles away, life on the farm and in the village was probably less visibly affected. Chittenden's statement about the scarcity of money, the plentitude of work and the barriers of distance are explained in the statement that "thus the whole of life revolved in a very small circle".

6 The hills of the "Southern Tier" are still covered by a fine stand of timber. The dense forests of Chittenden's day, however, are gone and in their place is a luxuriant second growth of hemlock, maple and birch.

7 Though the "sugar bush" can still be found in the back country of

western New York and the maple products are on a par with the vaunted
output of Vermont, the time and labor required by this rural industry
are slowly discouraging the ancient arts of "sugaring-off".

8 William Fletcher Chittenden, the author's father, born September 5,
1835, served as a private soldier in the Civil War.

9 Mary Jane (Wheeler) Chittenden, the author's mother, was born January
16, 1836. In the Chittenden collection is a copy of *The Yellowstone
National Park*, 1915 edition, which is inscribed "To Father and Mother
in honor of their 79th birthdays from their son Hiram author of the
book. April 4, 1915".

10 The Civil War, being so close in time and place, had its great influence
on the author. Among the Chittenden papers is an account concerning
Civil War casualties. Many of the instructors the author had as a
cadet at West Point embellished classroom lectures with first-hand
accounts of Civil War actions.

11 Franco-Prussian War of 1870.

12 Chittenden's interest in poetry, written and consumed, extended
throughout his life. His diaries contain numerous examples of the
romantic, Victorian type and make us thankful that he directed his
literary talents toward prose history. A privately printed volume of
poems, issued in 1916, is all that ever made its way into print.

13 Toward the end of Ulysses S. Grant's first term as president a vigorous
reform movement, growing out of public dissatisfaction with conditions
in the South, and with the low tone of public morality, developed into a
new Liberal Republican Party. At their convention in May 1872,
delegates adopted a platform condemning the administration of Grant,
demanding an end to restrictions on the South, and urging civil service
reform. Horace Greeley, eccentric editor of the New York *Tribune*,
was nominated on the Liberal Republican ticket. Even with the backing
of Southern Democrats, Greeley polled only 66 electoral votes to Grant's
286. Greeley died less than a month after the election, broken by the
abusive compaign and his decisive defeat. (Canfield-Wilder: *The Making
of Modern America* p. 454).

14 The Erie Railroad came through Cattaraugus County as early as 1851.
Short, connecting lines to the small towns (such as the State Line to
Ellicottville, built in 1878) were added in the twenty years following
the coming of the Erie.

15 Jacob Riis: *The Making of an American*. Riis was a Danish immigrant
whose books on various ethnic groups in America (such as *How the
Other Half Lives*) did much to point up the problems created by

national migrations to America which resulted in such evils as existed in New York City in the late 19th century. These were the problems of segregation which, in 1890, found New York City to be composed of "an Irish West Side, a German East Side, a 'Little Italy', a Chinatown, and sections that were mostly Russian, Polish or Greek". Under these conditions the process of Americanization became more difficult.

16 The last sentence in Chittenden's "Personal Notes", written, as the entire manuscript is, in his own hand, trails off in the middle of a sentence. This, apparently, was the last writing that Chittenden performed. All other papers in the Chittenden collection appear to have been dictated to his daughter, Eleanor Chittenden Cress.

Selected References

Blanchet, Francis Norbert: *Historical Sketches of the Catholic Church in Oregon* (Portland, 1878)

Bryce, George: *The Remarkable History of the Hudson's Bay Company* (New York, 1900)

Cleland, Robert Glass: *This Reckless Breed of Men: the trappers and fur traders of the Southwest* (New York, 1950)

De Smet, Pierre-Jean: *Letters and Sketches, 1841-42; The Oregon Missions* (Cleveland, 1906)

De Voto, Bernard: *Across the Wide Missouri* (Cambridge, 1947)

De Voto, Bernard: *The Course of Empire* (Cambridge, 1952)

Drumm, Stella M., ed.: *Journal of a Fur-Trading Expedition on the Upper Missouri, 1812-1813* (St. Louis, 1920)

Ermatinger, C. O.: *Hudson's Bay Company on the Columbia* (Washington Historical Quarterly, Vol. V, No. 3, pp. 192-206)

Ferris, Warren: *Life in the Rocky Mountains* (Denver, 1940)

Galbraith, J. S.: *The Hudson's Bay Company as an Imperial Factor.* (Berkeley 1957)

Gregg, Josiah: *Commerce of the Prairies* (Norman, Okla., 1944)

Hunter, Louis C.: *Steamboats on the Western Rivers: An Economic and Technological History* (Cambridge, 1949)

Hussey, John: *The History and Physical Structure of Fort Vancouver* (Tacoma, 1958)

Johansen and Gates: *Empire of the Columbia* (New York, 1957)

Kraus, Michael: *A History of American History* (New York, 1937)

Merk, Frederick: *Fur Trade and Empire* (Cambridge, 1931)

Morton, Arthur S.: *Sir George Simpson* (Portland, 1944)

Phillips, Paul C.: *The Fur Trade*, 2 vols. (Norman, Oklahoma, 1961)

Pilcher, Astor, Cass et al: *Report on the Fur Trade* (Senate Document 29, 21st Congress, 2nd Session, 1829)

Ross, Alexander: *Fur Traders of the Far West* (London, 1855)

Russell, Osborne: *Journal of a Trapper* (Portland, 1956)

Schenk, John Frederick: *The Hudson's Bay Company in Oregon* 1821-1860 (Master's Thesis, University of Oregon, 1932)

Shotwell, James T.: *The History of History* (New York, 1939)

Simpson, George: *Narrative of a Journey Around the World during the Years 1841 and 1842* (London, 1847)

Thompson, James Westfall: *History of Historical Writing* (New York, 1942)

Vestal, Stanley: *Mountain Men* (Boston, 1937)

Victor, Frances Fuller: *The River of the West* (Hartford, 1907)

Index

*A History of the American Fur Trade of
The Far West* 3, 7, 8, 9, 29, 79
Across the Wide Missouri 8
American Fur Company 3, 79, 82
American Society of Irrigation
Engineers 32
Angell, Norman 8
Arcade, New York 90, 108
Ashford, New York 90
Ashley, General W. H. 29, 53
Astorians 29, 47, 50, 83
Atlantic Monthly 8

Barry, J. Neilson 79
Bighorn Mountains 55, 70
Billington, Ray 8
Bonneville, Captain Benjamin 53
Bothwell, Albert J. 46-49
Bridger, James 29, 52
Burke, Thomas 8

Campbell, Robert 53
Cascade Tunnel 4, 9
Cattaraugus County, New York 87, 90
Century Magazine 8
Cheyenne,
Wyoming 41, 45, 50, 52, 54, 60, 68, 73
Chittenden, Clyde 97, 99, 100, 106
Chittenden, Hiram Martin
Not indexed, appears throughout
Chittenden, Hiram Martin, Jr. 7
Chittenden, Mary Jane Wheeler 9, 103
Chittenden Road 9, 13
Chittenden, Theodore P. 7
Chittenden, William 9, 103
Chouteau, Auguste 82
Chouteau, Pierre 82
Christian Science Monitor 8
Civil War 98
Cloud Peak Lake, Wyoming 54
Colorado Springs 32
Columbus, Ohio 21
Coues, Elliott 8, 81, 82, 83
Council Bluffs, Iowa 43
Cress, Eleanor Chittenden 7, 10, 20, 87
Cress, Major General James B. 13
Crowheart Butte, Wyoming 70
Cuba, New York 31

Day, John 79
Denver, Colorado 32, 44, 45, 67, 71
Devil's Gate, Wyoming 46, 47, 69
De Smet, Pierre-Jean 9
De Voto, Bernard 8

Ellicottville, New York 90
Entrance Arch, Yellowstone
National Park 13, 24-26
Estes Park, Colorado 70

Fort Collins, Colorado 60
Fort D. K. Russell, Colorado 52, 60
Fort John, Wyoming 52
Fort Laramie, Wyoming 29, 65, 69
Fort Meade, Wyoming 53
Fort McKinney, Wyoming 53
Fort Phil Kearny, Wyoming 54
Forum Magazine 8
Franklinville, New York 46, 90, 96

Gardiner, Montana 24, 26
Glacier National Park 7
Golden Gate Viaduct 13, 22
Greeley, Colorado 52
Greeley, Horace 105
Gros Ventre River 58

Hanford, Judge C. H. 7
Hay, Harry 55
Hayden, Ferdinand V. 44
Hemet Dam, California 37, 38, 39, 40
Hiram M. Chittenden Locks, Seattle 9
*History of Early Steamboat Navigation
on the Missouri River* 3, 7, 25, 83
Holmes, Justice Oliver Wendell 3
Huntington, Henry 39

Independence Rock 29, 47, 65, 69
Irrigation Congress 33, 67, 68
Irving, Washington 47
Irwin, Will 8

Jackson Hole, Wyoming 55, 59, 70, 72
Jones, Senator Wesley 8
Jordan, David Starr 8

Kansas City, Missouri 25, 26, 31, 51

Lake De Smet, Wyoming 54

Lane, Franklin 13
Laramie, Wyoming 45, 46, 60
Lareme, Joseph 53
Lewis and Clark Expedition 83
Lincoln, Abraham 98
Los Angeles, California 34, 39, 68
Louisville, Kentucky 21

Machias, New York 90, 105
Mammoth Hot Springs 16, 18
Mead, Elwood 32, 43, 54, 55, 56, 57,
  59, 68, 70, 72, 74
Missouri Historical Society 9
Missouri River Commission 3, 29, 67
Missouri Valley 7, 9, 79
Modesto, California 39
Mount Washburn 9, 13
Musket Lake, Idaho 59, 60, 72, 73

National Park Service 13
Nettleton, E. S. 55, 71
Newell, F. H. 33, 68
New York Herald Tribune 8
Nute, Grace Lee 8

Omaha, Nebraska 41, 43, 50
Oregon Trail 29, 49, 50, 65, 69
Osage River, Missouri 31
Owl Creek Mountains 57, 58

Palladino, Reverend L. B. 79
Phoenix, Arizona 32, 33, 34
Pickett, Colonel W. D. 57, 70
Pike, Zebulon 83
Pikes Peak, Colorado 32
Platte Reservoir, Colorado 44, 45
Powder River 54
Pratt, Parley 60

Reclamation Service 75
Richardson, A. T. 83
Richardson, F. M. 43
Riis, Jacob 107
Roosevelt, Theodore 4, 13, 22, 24, 25, 26

Salt Lake City, Utah 68
San Diego, California 34, 36, 68
Santa Fe, New Mexico 31, 32, 67
Sardinia, New York 90
Seabury, Samuel 8
Seattle, Port of 4, 7, 9, 10
Seddon, James A. 69, 74
Sedgwick, Ellery 8
Sheridan, Wyoming 52, 53, 54, 70
Silver Controversy 31

Sioux City, Iowa 13, 25
Snake River 59, 60
Southern Pacific Railroad 39
South Pass 83
Springville, New York 90
Stanford University 8
St. Louis, Missouri 3, 8, 25, 41, 43,
  50, 61, 69, 73, 79, 82
St. Louis *Republican* 82
St. Paul, Minnesota 15, 18, 19, 21
Sublette, Milton 29, 53
Sublette, William L. 29, 53
"Sugaring-off" 94
Sweetwater Valley, Wyoming 48

Tacoma, Washington 10
Taft, William Howard 10
Ten Broek Academy 41
*The Life, Letters and Travels of
  Father Pierre-Jean De Smet* 3, 7, 83
Tuolomne Dam, California 39
Turner, Frederick Jackson 8, 10

University of Washington 9
Upper Falls, Yellowstone
  National Park 13
Upper Missouri Historical Expedition 7
United States Army
  Corps of Engineers 3, 9, 10, 13, 15

Victor, Frances Fuller 40
Victor, Idaho 59

Wagner, W. F. 79
War or Peace 8
Washington State
  Historical Society 7, 9, 13
West Point, United States
  Military Academy 3, 7, 9, 47
Wheeler, Frank 92, 93
White River, Wyoming 53
Wilson, General John M. 21
Wind River 58, 70
Wind River Range 58
World War I 7, 8
Wright, C. C. 33, 34, 39
Wyeth, Nathaniel 53

Yellowstone National Park 3, 7, 9,
  13-26, 46, 48, 51, 59, 70
Yellowstone National Park (the book)
  8, 9, 13, 21, 22, 25, 81, 82
Yellowstone River 13, 54
Yorkshire, New York 9, 90

F   Chittenden, Hiram Martin, 1858-1917.
595   H.M. Chittenden; a western epic, being a selec-
C54   tion from his unpublished journals, diaries and
        reports. Edited with notes and introduction by
        Bruce Le Roy.   Tacoma, Washington State Histori-
        cal Society, 1961.
            viii, 136p. illus., ports., maps (on cover)
        26cm. index.
319265 "Of this regular edition ... one thousand
        copies have been printed."
            Bibliographical references included in "Foot-
        notes" (p.115-132) Bibliography: p.133-134.
1.The West-Descr. & trav.   2.Yellowstone National
Park. 3.Water conserva   tion-U.S. I.Le Roy, Bruce,
ed. II.Title.